THE
TAO
OF BUSINESS

Using ancient Chinese philosophy
to survive and prosper in times of crisis

Ansgar Gerstner

Translations from the *Daodejing* and *Zhuangzi*
by the author

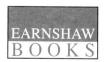
EARNSHAW
BOOKS

The Tao of Business
By Ansgar Gerstner

ISBN-13: 978-988-18154-7-7

© 2009 China Economic Review Publishing (HK) Limited for Earnshaw Books.

The Tao of Business is published by
China Economic Review Publishing (HK) Limited for Earnshaw Books
1804, 18/F New Victory House,
93-103 Wing Lok Street, Sheung Wan, Hong Kong

First printing August 2009
Second printing January 2010

This book has been set in 12pt Book Antiqua.

To my parents,
Rosemarie and Alex Gerstner

CONTENTS

执今之道
以御今之有

Grasp the Tao of the present
to handle the tasks of the present.

Chapter 1
Taoist Champions

Successful management

If you want your business to thrive and make substantial profits on a long-term basis, you need to build it on a truly healthy foundation. Successful management allows you to do exactly that. It generates remarkable revenues in good times, but – at least equally important – it also keeps your business profitable in times of crisis.

The one crisis on everybody's mind, while I have been writing *The Tao of Business* in 2008 and 2009, is of course the global financial meltdown. It is one of the topics addressed in this book, since it clearly shows that business managers today are far less concerned with the genuine long-term health of a company than they should be. Long-term corporate health does not come from a narrow focus on short-term profits. It needs a broader outlook.

Taoism has much to offer in this regard.

Taoism is known for its focus on individual well-being, and especially on the prevention of health problems. But less known is the fact that one of the major sources of Taoist wisdom, the *Daodejing*, has much to say about how to keep bigger organisms healthy long term and resilient in the face of crisis. The bigger organism the *Daodejing* is concerned with is the political state, but its lessons apply equally to modern business. In the book, I will show that the strategic advice offered by the *Daodejing* for more than 2,300 years can help you to put your business on a healthy and sound basis.

The simple word crisis can denote many different things. It does not exclusively refer to a large-scale global economic downturn. Your company, used to being the unchallenged market leader, might suddenly see itself threatened by the appearance of a strong competitor. Or maybe your company is confronted with new legal regulations, dramatic shifts in the market, lower demand, or a fierce price war started by one of your competitors.

There are all kinds of crises. Some can bring you to your knees and leave your business fighting for mere survival. But others might provide your company with unique opportunities to improve its position.

Take the market leaders in different industries and among diverse types and sizes of companies and look at their secrets of success, you will find certain elements repeated again and again. These businesses are typically strong in the following ways:

- They proactively seek out opportunities

- They work to anticipate and prevent problems.

- They are responsive to changes in their markets.

- They are far-sighted in reacting to socio-political developments and trends.

- They are highly flexible in addressing tasks.

These so-called secrets are well known and a huge amount has been written on them. What, then, can an ancient Chinese philosophy like Taoism offer to modern business besides these established truths?

When you look at the corporate culture and strategy of companies in a wide range of industries, you will find that often things are done in a piecemeal fashion. But running a long-term profitable business is like first-rate cooking. The real secret does not lie in the individual ingredients, although they have to be high class too. It rather is the perfect combination, sequence and timing and a broader perspective on how things fit into context that decide whether the outcome is average or first class.

Taoism is not about taking a piece here, taking a piece there and then simply putting them all in one pot. What Taoism is above all else is the glue that holds things together, a broad, coherent and holistic strategic perspective.

The *Daodejing* and the *Zhuangzi*

Taoism is one of Asia's major worldviews, and China's only indigenous faith. It has had enormous influence on the cultures of East Asia over the past 2,000 years, and its impact is increasingly felt beyond.

It is an approach to living rather than a systematic explanation of the origins of being. Taoism emphasizes compassion, spontaneity, and respect for nature. It calls for balance, and a oneness with life. It proposes that we should go with the natural flow of things, rather than resisting it.

The central text of Taoism is the *Daodejing* (*Tao Te Ching*), and legend holds that it was written by a person named Laozi (Lao Tse), supposedly an older contemporary of Confucius (551-479 B.C.). This book, a short five thousand characters in length, contains highly concentrated advice on how to live life, and particularly how to be a good leader. It appears to have been written primarily as a how-to manual for a ruler, and it is this aspect that makes it so relevant to the real rulers of the 21st century – the business elite.

As a modern business person, you would probably not expect a more than 2,000 year old book to address a subject that you wrestle with day after day — efficiency. But this is a recurrent theme in the *Daodejing*: how to achieve optimum results with minimum effort. The *Daodejing* offers some unexpected answers, at least for the Western mind.

Efficiency's chief ingredients, responsiveness and agility, also feature prominently in the *Daodejing*, being one of the reasons why this book and its lessons are so important in Chinese medicine, military strategic thought and the martial arts.

Taoism also draws inspiration from another philosopher who is supposed to have lived one or two centuries after the alleged author of the *Daodejing*, leaving to us a book known by his name, *Zhuangzi*.

Both, the *Daodejing* and the *Zhuangzi* give advice on how to live life properly. But unlike the *Daodejing*, the *Zhuangzi* does so through story-telling. There are stories like the famous butterfly dream which question black or white assumptions about reality, stories about making use of the useless, or about the relativity of knowledge.

Many of the stories describe people who

have arrived at exceptional levels in their respective fields. The book makes it clear, however, that to reach such levels of excellence, you need to possess more than mere professional skills. You need a philosophy, a strategy, a vision that gets you there.

The *Daodejing* and the *Zhuangzi* are the twin wells of wisdom from which all of Taoism springs, and they can provide the business person of today with a fresh outlook on corporate philosophy and strategy.

Taoist champions

Early Taoist writings contain stories of people living by drinking dew, climbing on clouds and riding flying dragons. These stories appear to us to be utterly fanciful. But they teach us an important lesson; not about how to attain super-natural powers, but about being open to realities beyond our immediate vision.

This is more important today than ever. The realities of people in different parts of the world and different walks of life and all their manifold work and life styles sometimes are so distant from each other, they almost seem as unreal to one another as are stories of ancient Taoist champions to modern readers.

Modern-day Taoist champions are aware of the coexistence of different realities. Managing different realities comes naturally to them and they know to productively link them together. They are not limited by a narrow vision of reality. Because of this, they are able to achieve extraordinary results.

The Taoists of ancient China were famous for their unconventional approach to life. They dressed and behaved differently. They claimed to be happy and more creative and open in their thinking as a result.

Modern Taoist champions are not limited in their thinking either. They are open to contemporary wisdom and practices. They are as comfortable with the Internet as they are with ancient wisdom. They fly across the world to attend business conferences, but also practice meditation and Tai Chi. They feel at home both in the middle of a buzzing city and in the seclusion of nature. They are very much in harmony with their emotions, intellect and body. This is the free and easy approach of a Taoist champion: not excluding the modern world but embracing it in all ways.

Modern Taoist champions have a very broad horizon. They are absolute experts in their respective fields, but the exact opposite of specialists suffering from tunnel vision. They are, in short, the 21st century versions of the Taoist sages of ancient times.

The Tao and the leader

What does *Tao* mean? At its most basic, the word Tao simply translates as path. But the meaning of the word extends well beyond that. In Taoism, the word Tao is a comprehensive philosophical concept. For Taoists, Tao is the base of all existence.

According to modern research, the *Daodejing* was probably compiled and written down in the fourth century BC, and was of course framed in the cultural and historical context of that era. China at the time was not China at all, but a series of states that were constantly at war with each other. To be a ruler of one of these states was to carry a heavy burden. They needed help, and the philosophers of the time stepped up and expounded on the rules for effective management of a state.

What is fascinating about the *Daodejing* is that in terse, concentrated statements, it expresses both general principles and delivers operational advice. The *Daodejing* is of course not about doing business. It was written primarily for political leaders, and key sections are therefore about the art of leadership. Regardless of its original intended readers, its advice is as valuable today as it was more than 2,300 years ago.

The *Daodejing*'s references to "the leader" would have been assumed at the time to mean a man, but in fact according to Chinese grammar it is gender non-specific. As a result, as you read this book, remember that the business leader being referred to could be either male or female.

The *Daodejing* takes a pragmatic view of the world, and stresses the need for balance and harmony in all things. It says that balance and harmony are catalysts for efficiency. It advocates social and environmental responsibility. It recommends that human and natural energies and resources should be handled with care.

In this book, I will try to show that this all makes good business sense, and that the Tao is not just a vague philosophical concept, but a promising path to success in business.

善建者不拔
善抱者不脱

Something that is well established
cannot be uprooted.

Chapter 2
Building a Business

The action of non-action

Probably the most famous term in Taoism, aside from the Tao itself, is *wuwei,* which is often translated as "do nothing" or "non-action". But it really means being in tune with your surroundings, understanding all aspects of yourself, and going with the flow – taking action or doing nothing as a natural extension of the situation.

For the *Daodejing* and the *Zhuangzi,* there is a deeper structure to the affairs of the universe. Not in a religious way, more like gravity. The Tao of the *Daodejing* is not about the belief in a god of any kind. It is about a belief in nature, a belief in the fundamental rightness of natural processes.

Taoism believes in a kind of self-organizing system, that there are patterns to the world and its affairs, and that it is best to let these patterns operate without interference. The world is at its best when natural patterns are allowed to operate smoothly. The same is true of situations, problems, people and even businesses.

Wuwei is closely linked with this idea. In order to be able to apply *wuwei* – to "act by not acting" (*Daodejing*, chapter 63) – you need good intuition and instinct and be excellent at sensing what is going on.

In business as in other areas of life, you may sometimes have a strange feeling. You are in a meeting. The numbers look fine, the manager is saying all the right things. But your instinct is telling you there is something wrong.

You are looking at a new strategic partnership. The prospective business partner is ideal in all ways that can be listed and enumerated, but your gut tells you to check things again.

Learn to trust your instinct. You constantly face situations requiring quick decisions. Be calm, look within yourself, follow the Tao, and make your choice.

Of course, not everyone is equally able

to do so. Depending on personality and up-bringing some people perceive and foresee the tiniest details while others tend to neglect what their inner voices are telling them. If you belong to the latter group, work to get back in touch with your instincts and intuition.

There is no simple answer as how to achieve this, no fast solution. It can be done in a number of different ways, both Eastern or Western. Choose the method that is most suitable for you. Traditional Chinese ways to get in better touch with one's instincts and in-tuition include calligraphy, music, meditation and the martial arts. These disciplines focus on being "one" with the flow of life, and the routines that are part of the training help you to get into that flow.

In a *wuwei* state of mind you sense what is the best course of action, and in many cases, the best action may be no action at all.

Warren Buffett, one of the world's richest men for many years, is a perfect example of a successful business man who understands the power of refraining from action. He is not in-terested in hopping around and shopping for short-term yields. Instead, he is paying much attention to consistent long-term results.

Like an advanced Kung Fu practitioner, Buffett is less concerned with fast-changing developments than with solid ground rules, trends and strategies. The secret of Warren Buffett's success lies not in the complexity of his approach, but in its highly efficient simplicity. It is about focusing and reduction.

Chapter 60 of the *Daodejing* includes the following quote: "Managing a large country is like cooking a small fish." Too much commotion, too much stirring can ruin a delicate affair.

In a talk at the University of Florida School of Business, Warren Buffett gave a classic piece of "Taoist" advice to students on how to succeed at investment: "Wall Street makes money on activity. You make money on inactivity."

Pushing too hard in a certain direction or putting too much will into a decision, can blind you to essential elements of the process. If you ignore those elements, your decisions may be doomed to failure or at least cause significant trouble. It sounds paradoxical, but sometimes you get more done by doing less.

This can be particularly tough for Westerners, who are used to dealing with situations by taking action. But Westerners will be pleased to hear that the opposite is also true. That is, to take no action where a situation requires it, where a process needs to be moved in a more natural direction, will likewise result in more trouble.

So *wuwei* can be either action or non-action, whatever helps a process to be in harmony with the overall situation. It depends on the circumstances, and that is where instinct and intuition come in.

However, we cannot rely on intuition and instinct alone. Our decisions also need to be rooted in sound knowledge. The question is how wide the scope of our knowledge is and how we can reach beyond it.

A telling example can be found in innovation. Innovations often develop in completely unpredictable paths before they achieve financial success. Charles Leadbeater, a leading authority on innovation and creativity, provided fascinating insights into this in a TED speech in 2005, showing that many success stories do not originate from the brains of Research & Development specialists in large companies spending huge amounts of money looking for new trends and potentially best-selling products. They are invented by dedicated users.

In his speech, Leadbeater told the story of the mountain bike and its development by a group of young people in California dissatisfied with the bicycles available to them at the time. They started to assemble the kinds of bicycles they would want for themselves, combining the frames of ordinary bikes, the gears of racing bikes and brakes from motorbikes. After a couple of years, a small business saw the opportunity and started selling these specialized bikes, but it still took another ten to fifteen years before the big bicycle companies began to see mass market potential and mountain bikes really became mainstream.

In his 2006 report, *The User Innovation Revolution*, Leadbeater suggests that companies can largely improve their Research & Development if they more effectively tap into and integrate the knowledge and creativity of users and consumers.

This is a more open approach to professional knowledge – where it comes from and where to find it – and also an intelligent way to widen a company's knowledge base, to enhance its relationship with customers, strengthen customer loyalty and stay in tune with the pulse of the times. Allow things to happen and apply *wuwei*. Acknowledge the limits of your own knowledge, but do not allow these limits to limit you.

Nassim Taleb, a long-time derivatives trader and currently a professor of risk engineering, gives what in effect is Taoist advice about embracing one's own limitations. In *The Black Swan*, a book about the impact of randomness on the financial markets, he explains that many companies overrate their competence in terms of risk assessment and control, something that has become obvious in the many large companies that stumbled during the current economic crisis. In the *Daodejing* it says: "It is good to know what you don't know. But it is a deficiency to not know what you do not know." (Chapter 71)

It is very human to believe that we know more than we actually do and to act on the basis of this false premise. But it can be very dangerous, even fatal, for a business. You have to be careful to recognize the limitations of your knowledge and not interfere with processes in the false belief that you completely understand a situation and can predict precisely the outcome of a certain action.

This is a call to avoid arrogance and conceit and to recognize the danger of imposing one's will on a situation when a more reactive and inclusive attitude would be wiser. This is *wuwei*. When you are really in touch with yourself, you will clearly know your own strengths and limitations.

The Taoist concept of *wuwei* also underpins the Chinese martial arts. Good Chinese Kung Fu fighters make more use of their opponents' weaknesses than their own strengths. It is a process that is based more on instinct than on force. A good fighter acts and reacts in perfect unison with the demands of a situation.

With many decisions, it is not enough to be smart and to have access to large amounts of relevant, or seemingly relevant, information. Data might be contradictory and different sources might provide you with differing analyses of the current situation and varying forecasts of future developments.

In this age of high technology, in which the absolute certainties of 1 and 0 rule both our computer processes and our lives, some people feel that instinct and intuition are somehow primitive and unreliable. That there should be a program, or an MBA textbook method, that will resolve all problems.

The assumption is: create to do lists to organize your life properly and all will be well. Well, it won't.

You can use Google to gather information, but you cannot use Google to make a decision. For that you must turn inside, absorb the information, consider the issues, trust yourself and take a leap of faith on the wings of instinct and reason.

Trust

"If you do not have enough trust in yourself and others, people will have no trust in you." (*Daodejing*, chapter 17)

Steve Jobs, co-founder and CEO of Apple, is not someone you would necessarily think of as a Taoist. Yet he is proof of the significance of trusting one's inner voice and intuition.

As Jobs said in a commencement speech at Stanford University in 2005, he dropped out of college after only a couple of months, trusting that everything would work out well. He stayed on at college as a "drop-in" for another year or so, during which time he attended a course on calligraphy, immersing himself in something seemingly impractical and unprofitable. But this class in calligraphy has definitely paid off for Apple. Apple has become well known for its designs and for its blending of aesthetics with function.

Chapter four of the *Zhuangzi* says: "Everybody knows about the use of something useful, but hardly anybody knows about the use of something not useful." To see – or better, to sense – potential in seemingly useless things and actions, you must not be too much concerned with immediate applicability and benefit. But you need to have complete trust in your choices.

Trust is a crucial part of business. But trust is not something that can be written into a contract. It cannot be nailed down or quantified. It is built upon instinct and survives through careful intuitive tending.

One of the great clichés of China business is *guanxi* – the importance of relationships. And while *guanxi* is a cliché, it is also true that Chinese business people in general spend more time and put more emphasis on the underlying feel of a business relationship, and less on the contract.

The Western businessman typically wants a contract as thick as a telephone directory, which includes clauses that deal with all eventualities in a black and white manner. He wants to sign this massive document, then go back to the hotel and watch a DVD.

The Chinese businessman, on the other hand, prefers a contract of two pages. He wants to sign a simple general agreement, then go to a karaoke club.

The point of karaoke is not the singing, which is almost always awful. It is getting to know your partners. The Chinese businessman knows that if there is trust, then they will find a way together through whatever problems arise. He also knows that if there is no trust, then it does not matter how many clauses are added to the contract. The relationship and the project will fail.

Provide benefit rather than do harm

Nature is the primary model for Taoist thought. Above all, it is the continuity and the cyclical processes found throughout nature that figure so prominently in Taoist thinking. For instance, think of the sun and the moon, of water and of the four seasons. Taoists appreciate their life-giving qualities, and prefer processes which are in tune with these huge forces of nature, which are beneficial to all parties involved and sustainable long-term.

The *Daodejing* says: "Superior people are

like water, benefiting all beings without competing with them." (Chapter 8)

At first sight, it might look like there is not much of a connection with business. Look more closely, however, and you will see that there is huge business potential in such ideas. For instance, there is no "win-lose" perspective in the Taoist mindset. Taoism is about creating sustainable long-term "win-win" environments. And what better business outcome is there than "win-win"?

Aiming at "win-win" situations – not only for yourself and your business partners, but also for your employees and even for society – provides payback in many different ways.

You benefit, for example, if you are able to create a workplace where people are not only in it for the monthly salary but where they also enjoy what they are doing, where they have opportunities to learn and develop, where they see that using their initiative and applying their creativity is really appreciated and encouraged.

Choosing this Taoist approach, you can build a really strong team of committed staff who will help you in all ways. The people in such a team do not need to be pushed to work. It comes naturally to them because they see that there is meaning for themselves and for others in what they do. With an enthusiastic team, the work is more enjoyable, more things happen more smoothly, more opportunities are created and acted upon more effectively.

When you build or lead a business, it is your choice, and your choice alone, as to what atmosphere you create and spend most of your days in.

Other good examples of "win-win" situations are environmental protection and corporate social responsibility. There are people who think that social responsibility and "green" awareness are incompatible with a profitable business. But as many companies can show, this is not true. It is entirely possible to make money and at the same time to act in a socially and environmentally responsible way.

Especially in the field of environmental protection, providing broader benefits to society and making profits can go very well together. A growing ecological awareness creates plenty of green business opportunities, not only for small to medium-sized companies.

Even big companies such as Siemens and Bosch, who certainly were not among the first to enthusiastically embrace green ideas, are now investing heavily in envirotech. As recently stated by the German business news magazine *Wirtschaftswoche*, Siemens now makes 19 billion Euros, about a quarter of its turnover, through green technology and they are aiming to make it 25 billion Euros by 2011.

Bosch, which so far only makes a very small percentage of its turnover from renewable energy, spent one billion Euros to buy Ersol Solar Energy and plans to invest another half a billion Euros till the year 2012 to produce solar cells in a manufacturing plant in Eastern Germany. Bosch simply sees the necessity to reduce its heavy dependence on the conventional automotive industry.

Or take "green" IT and high tech. There is enormous demand for energy efficient computers, servers and appliances that help reduce costs.

A 2007 joint study by the German Institute for Economic Research, the Fraunhofer Institute and Roland Berger Strategy Consultants, sees dynamic world-wide economic growth potential in environmental protection. By 2030 it expects environmental technologies in Germany alone to generate 1 trillion Euros in revenue as compared to 570 billion by the automotive industry. To give you some comparative figures: In Germany in 2005, environmental technologies generated 150 billion and the automotive industry 280 billion Euros in revenue.

In chapter 7 of the *Daodejing* you can read: "Heaven and Earth have existed for a long time. The reason heaven and earth can exist for so long is that they do not live for themselves alone."

A clearly un-Taoist point of view that has set the trend for quite a while is Milton Friedman's position that the sole social responsibility of a company is to increase its own profits. Friedman was one of the most influential economists of the 20th century and received the Nobel Prize for economic sciences in 1976.

Of course, without profits a company cannot survive, and a prerequisite for any long-term social responsibility that a company can assume is its survival. But it makes a difference whether, besides the profitable management of your business, you also recognize wider responsibilities within a local and global socio-political context.

Bill Gates, former CEO of Microsoft, could never be accused of being a flower power idealist. He is a hard-nosed and highly competitive businessman. But he also strongly argues for corporate philanthropy and the foundation he launched in 1994 with his wife Melinda is working to reduce poverty and improve healthcare on a worldwide scale.

In a speech given by Gates at the World Economic Forum 2008 in Davos, Switzerland, entitled "A New Approach to Capitalism in the 21st Century", he asks companies to allow some of their best minds to allocate time to help solving the world's worst problems. He even goes so far as to suggest a new form of capitalism which he calls "creative capitalism" in which businesses, governments and NGOs work together to reduce the inequities of the world.

Many successful business people and entrepreneurs worldwide establish their own foundations, support their local communities or do something to help solve urgent problems like poverty and hunger.

Bo Burlingham's *Small Giants: Companies that Choose to Be Great Instead of Big*, a finalist for the 2006 Financial Times and Goldman Sachs Business Book of the Year award, provides inspiring examples of very successful private businesses for which profit is not everything. All of the companies presented in the book are excellent in their specific profession. They are passionate about what they do and they genuinely care for people. They do not only look after their employees, but after all of their businesses' stakeholders including the communities they are operating in.

In business in general, there seems to be a gradual shift away from Milton Friedman's doctrine of "profit is everything".

Environmental concerns and issues of corporate social responsibility increasingly weigh on public opinion. As a 2007 global McKinsey survey points out, companies feel these pressures and know they have to respond.

Some companies are serious about societal issues, while others have their marketing and PR departments handle them and do not truly make them an integral part of their corporate culture. If you and your company ignore societal issues while your competitors pay attention to them, then you risk damage both to your reputation and to your revenues.

Constancy

"To know how to be constant is true intelligence. Not to know how to be constant is arbitrariness. Arbitrary behavior brings disaster." (*Daodejing*, chapter 16)

Sustainability and constancy are closely interlinked concepts in the *Daodejing*. Individual profit at the expense of others or at the expense of the environment is clearly against the spirit of the Tao.

To achieve constancy it is very important to choose the right people to work with – be it your own team, business partners or clients. But in order to find the right people, you have to offer something to them that makes them want to work with you long term. Many people are too much concerned about their own needs and goals, and spend too little time thinking about what they can offer others in return for helping them to achieve goals, aside from money, which is only one among many reasons for accepting a job, a project or a business relationship.

"Something that is established well cannot be uprooted. Something that is firmly embraced cannot be taken away. The children and grandchildren will not stop the ancestral worship." (*Daodejing*, chapter 54)

This is another quote showing the Taoist emphasis on long-term perspectives, also for coming generations. It makes a huge difference for strategic planning as to whether you mainly focus on short-term results and immediate profit maximization, or whether you also consider the effect that measures taken today might have in terms of a wider context, both now and in the future.

Easily overlooked in this context is the importance of long-term leadership. Of course, constancy in leadership does not guarantee farsighted management decisions. Nothing does. But it helps, as has been proven by what Hermann Simon, a German management consultant and former professor for management and marketing, calls *hidden champions*. Hidden champions are small to medium-sized companies that do not appear on public radar, but are European or worldwide technology or market leaders. Like Burlingham's *small giants*, they are privately owned and therefore more easily under long-term leadership. But even if your company does not fall into this category, it is still possible to make sustainable leadership an essential part of your corporate culture and be pleased with its positive effects.

Management guru Jim Collins, author of the bestselling book *Good to Great*, gives a good description of really sustainable leadership. Great CEOs, he says, do not only lead their companies to great success during their tenure. Their true greatness lies in shaping and structuring company and corporate culture to the effect that for a long period after their departure, their companies still operate successfully. This point deserves special attention, since many companies tend to fade once their "mastermind" leaves.

Reduction

"Practicing the Tao, you reduce day by day. You reduce and reduce again, to eventually arrive at non-action." (*Daodejing*, chapter 48)

The Taoist path is to make things simple. The focus in the *Daodejing* is not on "adding", it is on "reducing".

The *Daodejing*'s concept of reduction first of all applies to *all* kinds of activities and processes. But in a narrow sense, it is an idea closely linked with leadership, since it is defined in terms of the qualities of good leaders. Chapter 48 continues: "With non-action nothing stays undone. The world is conquered by having no [personal] agenda. Someone with a [personal] agenda is not qualified to take over the world."

What matters is the objective of a project and its accomplishment in the most efficient way. Personal ambition in a leader is seen as hampering this process.

The kind of reduction the *Daodejing* talks about aims at non-action. Done right, it eventually leads to smooth "movements". Processes that are running smoothly cause less friction and result in less attrition. The point is to make optimal use of available resources and to enhance efficiency by cutting out invasive and superfluous actions.

It is often the fear of losing control that makes people add issues and complexities to a situation. But the fact is that overall, you are more likely to be in control if you reduce interference, and focus instead on effective communication and cooperation.

Reduction, in the *Daodejing,* is about an increase in quality. It is a concept that can be applied in many different ways.

If you are overseeing a business, your daily "To-Do" list is probably overflowing with items. You do not need more responsibilities and issues, but that is exactly what you will get if you are either too autocratic or too loose in your style of management. The aim should be to reduce and simplify that "To- Do" list, not lengthen it.

Going too far in either direction – too much control, too little control – also creates discontent amongst employees who feel that their capabilities and suggestions are not appreciated, or that they lack either direction or a chance to play a full role. Discontented employees create unnecessary problems, inefficiencies and costs. Discontented employees can also create dissatisfied customers, which directly threatens your business.

Often the problem is not that things are complicated. Some situations are complicated, in which case you should approach them as interesting challenges. But very often, processes have not been structured well and are more complex than they need to be. Keeping things simple is an art. And, as with any art, simplicity needs to be cultivated.

Chapter 2

Building a Business

Tao Takeaways

- 🌀 Trust your instincts and intuition
- 🌀 Be proactive - Taoism is NOT about inactivity
- 🌀 Trust is more important than contract clauses
- 🌀 Emphasize sustainability
- 🌀 Build for the long-term
- 🌀 Look for "win-win" situations
- 🌀 Make full use of your potential

天下莫柔弱于水
而攻坚强者莫之能胜
以其无以易之

Nothing is weaker than water.
Nothing has greater power
to attack the strong.

Chapter 3

Competing in the Marketplace

Non-competitive competitiveness

"The Tao of heaven is not to compete, but to be good at winning." (Daodejing, chapter 73)

Reading through the *Daodejing*, you will find that a non-competitive attitude is always emphasized and favored. Would it be better to write off this way of thinking as out of date? Or is it possible to profit from such an attitude even in today's highly competitive business environments? And if so, how?

The passages in the *Daodejing* which talk about competing are always about getting the job done in a way that multiplies positive side effects. The reason for this is simple. Side effects, no matter whether negative or positive, have a natural tendency to spread, often causing very complex and no longer controllable chain reactions.

Keeping this in mind is important in a business context. Business practices aimed overall at creating positive side effects have a direct impact on the competitiveness of your business or organization.

Look at it like this. There are many different ways to compete. Each way triggers its own specific chain of reactions. With a "win-lose" mindset, for instance, you can only be either on the winning side or the losing side. This mindset itself creates losers. A completely different approach is the "win-win" frame of mind. You still aim at winning, but you do so by looking for situations and deals in which not only you but all parties can profit.

Take the example of Apple and Microsoft in 1997. Apple was in trouble and in a highly confrontational situation with Microsoft. Steve Jobs of Apple recognized that a "win-lose" mindset is destructive to a business, especially if you are in a weaker position than your competitor.

At the 1997 MacWorld, Jobs announced a new cooperation with Microsoft in his keynote speech and Bill Gates addressed the audience via satellite link. As Jobs explained ten years later in a joint interview with Gates, instead of continuing the fight against Microsoft in 1997, he looked for new ways of cooperation and Apple emerged all the stronger.

There is additional "return on investment" to be had if you ally with partners or businesses not only with your own interests in mind, but also with the interests of others. Besides enhancing your personal credibility, you will find people more willing to work for you and more likely to offer you information which you might otherwise not have access to. This leads in turn to new opportunities.

Taoist non-competitive competitiveness is about inclusiveness and openness. Taoists see power tussles as being ultimately destructive for all and reflective of self-conceit and a blindness to the potential at hand. Taoists embrace diversity.

Indra Nooyi, CEO of PepsiCo, listed number 1 in *Fortune Magazine*'s "50 Most Powerful Women in Business" in 2006, 2007 and 2008, is clearly aware of the business potential of diversity and of its role in PepsiCo's growth under her leadership.

In a interview with the *DiversityInc* magazine in May 2008, Indra Nooyi points out that when she became CEO, diversity had already been well established as part of PepsiCo's business strategy and that she is pushing forward on this path. She says, "I'm not your normal non-diverse CEO." Being Indian born and female, and also the head of a Fortune 500 company, she sees herself as vivid living proof of her company's understanding of the issue of diversity.

Reluctance to embrace diversity – particularly visible in the percentage of males and females or of people of different ethnic and linguistic origin in the top management of a company – is often the result of ignorance and conceit. It is obviously imprudent to miss out on talent by ignoring large segments of the population and rejecting good people who are then available to be hired by competitors.

Your company has a much more intelligent and efficient substructure if your workforce, from the lowest to highest strategic positions, is somehow reflective of the gender, ethnic and age composition of your customer base. This will make it easier to understand the logic, needs and aspirations of your possibly different groups of customers and to anticipate future trends.

Taoist decision makers know of the multi-level benefits of non-competitive competitiveness. The *Daodejing* (in chapter 22) says: "Sages do not show off, therefore they shine. They are not self-opinionated, therefore they are distinguished. They do not boast of themselves, therefore they have merit. They are not arrogant, therefore they are leaders. Because they do not compete, no one in the world is able to compete with them."

The *Daodejing* emphasizes *not competing*, or *not getting into confrontational situations.* Preventing confrontation always makes sense strategically. Situations involving emotional conflict give rise to anger, frustration, and the desire to obstruct or retaliate. People get aggressive. They tend to act against your wishes, explicitly or implicitly, consciously or unconsciously.

Tai Chi offers us a good example of Taoist non-competitive competitiveness. In the Tai Chi "pushing hands" exercise, you make optimum use of incoming force to enhance your own strength.

When you watch two Tai Chi masters do pushing hands, you can observe that the softer, more supple, and at the same time better "grounded" one of the two is able to push his counterpart backwards seemingly without effort. The same skills and concepts can be helpful in negotiating deals.

The standard logic of "you push and I push back" does not generally provide you with the best possible results. A "win-win" frame of mind, however, creates situations that are emotionally much more satisfying. You then profit on several levels.

A good warrior is not hot-tempered

"A good military commander is not aggressive. A good warrior is not hot-tempered. A good winner does not jostle. Someone who is good at employing people places himself below them. This is called the *De* of not-competing. This is called making use of other people's strengths. This is called complying with heaven." (*Daodejing*, chapter 68)

In times of ever tougher competition, there is increasing pressure on businesses of all sizes, from multinational to local. Strategies that might have worked for decades, work no longer. So companies and the people who run them need to be flexible and actively seek out, or create, new competitive advantages.

The intense drive for results and for cost control, sometimes even the necessity to fight for survival, puts additional pressure on managers and business owners. To make good decisions under stress you need to stay calm, relaxed and open-minded. This sounds obvious, but it takes a mature personality to act like this. It requires hard work. Someone who is easily irritable and hot-tempered is likely to misjudge situations, and to make premature and costly decisions.

Regardless of whether you are discussing a business acquisition, planning a strategic shift or negotiating a salary package with an employee – you should not allow strong emotions, either your own or those of others, to affect your thinking and actions. Stay aware of group dynamics, pay attention to your communication skills and learn to stay cool in tense circumstances. Be calm and objective in your assessments.

The challenge in any business situation is to make the right choice. Strong emotions and subjectivity do not help. Let the decisions naturally flow from the information available, and where the information available is insufficient to reach a clear decision, trust your instinct and your intuition, just like a good warrior does.

Harmony

"To harmonize is called constancy. To know how to harmonize is true intelligence." (*Daodejing*, chapter 55)

The word "harmony" tends to sound flat to many people because it is so overused. Seen in the context of interpersonal interactions, it often evokes the image of a weak guy looking to avoid conflict. In the *Daodejing*, however, harmony is not a hollow concept. It means being in touch with yourself and the environment, knowing how to get along with people and situations, in order to get things done in a positive and lasting way. The *Daodejing* does not talk about a state of harmony. Instead, it focuses on creating and maintaining harmony which is an ongoing process requiring continuous adaptation.

The term "to harmonize" works in two directions: One is internal – to be and to stay in sync with yourself and your surroundings. The other is external – to help people and situations around you to be more balanced. The ability to harmonize is essential for people in positions of responsibility. Of course, it is possible to be aggressive and harsh towards others and still be successful, at least in some respects. But if you want to be on top and create something meaningful and lasting, it is better to optimize your ability to listen to other people and cooperate with them.

In highly competitive environments, friction is inevitable. Therefore, it is important to have skills that will allow you to deal with such friction. Theoretical knowledge of people management is of little use. The key to handling such situations rests within yourself. The more you are in touch with yourself and your surroundings, the better you will be able to perform. The personality of the manager has a strong impact on how fast a team overcomes friction and achieves focus and equilibrium, or on how quickly a business relationship recovers from a dispute.

It is in times of real crisis, such as an economic downturn, that a company really shows what it is made of. A crisis can trigger irrational and hasty actions. Hence it is even more important to keep sight of measures that take into account the larger perspective and are not simply reactive quick fixes to the latest bad news.

Consider the case of Southwest Airlines. Once, when faced with tough times in its early years – Southwest Airlines started operations in 1971 – the company sold an aircraft rather than lay off people. After 9/11, when about 100,000 of the 500,000 airline employees in the

United States were laid off, Southwest Airlines laid off none. The company used its creativity and made cuts in other places. Not laying off employees did not weaken it. On the contrary, Southwest turned a profit in 2001 and 2002, unlike other US airlines that filed huge losses. Thanks to these Taoist moves, it also strengthened its reputation.

This is a strategy that of course does not fit all circumstances. Sometimes economic and political conditions are such that a company would not survive without laying off people, and such behaviour would not be non-Taoist, because it might be the only way to preserve the corporate organism.

Layoffs can be necessary and efficient in some industry sectors and under certain political and economical conditions. But as a general tool to cut costs, they often represent a focus on short-term results instead of on organic growth in a long-term perspective.

As Darrell Rigby of Bain & Company points out, large-scale downsizing in an economic downturn can be an indicator of operational and strategic weakness, eventually revealing problems that have had a more or less silent existence in the background for some time.

Depending on how long a crisis lasts and on how fast you have to rehire employees, there are many costs that can offset the short-term wage savings of layoffs. Apart from an increased workload for other staff, layoffs can also result in low morale and diminished performance with the remaining workforce.

Also to be considered are the time, energy and money that need to be expended once the crisis is over, on the search for new talent, on training and making teams productive and operations smooth again, before your company reaches its original levels of efficiency, performance and competitiveness. Calculations by Bain & Company in Boston show that layoffs pay off financially only if positions remain vacant for at least six months.

Look at harmony from another angle: sports. Without a good team you are not going to win the game. But what is a good team? Even if the individual members of a team are world class, this does not guarantee that the team will be world class.

Strong individuals have a tendency to do things their own way. To be the leader of a team, you must be able to harmonize. You need the ability to listen well, to sense what is going on beneath the surface, to speak out clearly and to define boundaries. When you are in sync with yourself, handling issues in a cooperative and communicative style, you can do all this and more in a way that is inspirational, that boosts the team spirit and gets results.

In business to business interactions, you also need more than just reliable partners, thorough knowledge of the market and of factors that might give you a competitive advantage. As you will not be dealing with the abstract notion of a business, but with real individuals, your personality and approach to people and tasks becomes an essential part of the cocktail, and might be decisive in terms of the success or failure of the cooperation.

Soft skills tend to get neglected in a world of hard facts and tough decisions. But they can give you a clear competitive advantage. As a result, personal growth is vital for people in management positions. Self-awareness, openness and the ability to listen and to communicate well are all critical for the success of a manager.

Agility

"Nothing in the world is softer and weaker than water, but in terms of its ability to attack the firm and the strong, nothing can surpass it. This is because there is nothing that can change it." (*Daodejing*, chapter 78)

What makes water "invincible" is that nothing can change its inherent quality of utmost adaptability and agility. In this respect, water serves as an interesting model for management. You know how difficult it is to always stay both relaxed and agile, especially in the course of demanding situations. It requires continuous awareness and effort.

Agility is a quality that is very much needed today. Accelerated globalization and the Internet are transforming our lives and make many familiar attitudes and approaches obsolete. The speed with which things change makes agility a necessity if you want to succeed.

In a business context this means you need to do quite a bit of lifestyle maintenance, establishing procedures and strategies that allow you to monitor behavior and avoid rigidity. What has worked in the past or in one country might not work today or in another culture. This sounds obvious, but many companies do not pay enough attention to this in their day-to-day operations or simply prefer to stick to old recipes. A strategy sometimes works even if it seems a bit outdated and less than ideal. But it can be dangerous if you are too slow and too inflexible to react to changes in the market – especially if your competitors are versatile.

Some large companies with an inflated bureaucracy and a lack of flexibility can still make money, at least for a while. They live off the past, off a solid foundation laid by capable people in days gone by and a reputation earned long ago. But inflexibility is dangerous for any company, large or small. The willingness to embrace change is fundamental.

One such agent of change was Andrea

Jung, CEO of Avon Products and number 19 on *Forbes Magazine*'s "The 100 Most Powerful Women" 2008 list. She succeeded in transforming a rather fusty company with more than a century of history that had lost its edge back into a thriving business.

When she became Avon's CEO in 1999, sales were down sharply and so was the share price. After a lot of restructuring, introduction of more efficient technologies and process streamlining and by extending Avon's product reach to teenagers and college-age women, "The Company for Women" turned agile and hip again.

Flexibility and the ability to quickly adapt to changing situations can overcome almost any obstacle. The *Daodejing* says: "The softest in the world can make use of the hardest in the world. That which is without existence can penetrate that which is without an opening." (Chapter 43)

In Taoism, as in Zen, the most important training routines for attaining mastery are not forms of self-cultivation set apart from your "ordinary" life, such as meditation, but rather all of the sometimes trivial, sometimes complex tasks with which we are confronted daily in our professional and private lives, and the way in which we handle them.

If you happen to have a child, then you have a wonderful personal trainer of the Tao right at home. Infants are important teachers, according to the *Daodejing*. They are especially good at monitoring your flexibility. Looking after them, you will be constantly faced with annoyance and impatience, because they simply do not care to alter their behavior to best fit *your* plans and interests. They will interrupt you. You might be forced into doing things you had no intention of doing. Plans will have to be delayed and changed.

Ask yourself these questions: How flexible am I in reacting to such situations? What are my emotions? Do I react in a way that is reasonable? Are my expectations realistic? How much do interruptions and changes affect my efficiency in doing what I am doing? Do I really try to see things from the perspective of the child? To what extent can I benefit from interruptions and changes?

Apply comparable questions to customer service, and you might find that sometimes it is not the unreasonable requests of customers that strain your patience, so much as your own inflexible preconceived ideas of what your customers need, of how they are supposed to act.

If you want to provide good service and if you want to develop strong customer loyalty, you had better look at things from the perspective of your customers. What *you* think they want or what *you* think is reasonable for them to ask for, might differ significantly from what your customers are actually looking for and the services they see themselves as being entitled to.

Routines provide guidance and structure and result in accelerated processes. But this is only true if you handle them in a flexible way and always adapt them to the needs of specific tasks and individuals. Flexibility has a lot to do with intuition and instinct. You have to allow all parts of your personality to play a part in decision-making if you want to be fully equipped for all situations. And you should also encourage the same approach in all team members and staff.

It all starts in the mind. Make it a habit to constantly assess your own behavior. How do you rank on a scale from flexible to rigid? How do you react when members of your immediate team or other members of your staff present you with solutions they came up with themselves? Are you someone who thinks that you always know best? Or are you a person who is able to listen, to delegate and coordinate ideas and strategies to get the best possible results?

An effective way to maintain flexibility, and with it creativity, is to foster a learning culture in your business. This includes you, as the manager or business owner, as well as your team members or employees. Knowledge does not only flow from the top down. For best results, it has to spread in every direction. But this only happens if you allow it.

In complex environments, simple top-down directives without effective information flows in other directions do not allow for tasks to be handled in the best possible way. This is especially true when you are also dealing with different local or cultural contexts. Allowing the collective intelligence of all people involved to be brought to bear on a situation is often more effective and makes your company more flexible.

Remember that there is always a way to get things done, even if you sometimes seem to be at a dead end. The question is simply whether or not you are agile enough to adapt to all kinds of situations and find a better path.

The *Daodejing's* formulation is quite radical: "When people are born, they are soft and weak. When they are dead, they are firm and rigid. When plants start to sprout, they are soft and fragile. When they are dead, they are dry and withered. Therefore, the firm and rigid are followers of death. The soft and weak are followers of life." (Chapter 76)

Fix things before they become problems

"Act before it appears. Fix it, before there is a

mess." (*Daodejing*, chapter 64)

It is not hard to find examples of companies that failed to follow the Tao on that score. Anticipating difficulties and taking corrective action before problems get out of control can save money, increase revenue, make you more competitive and help you to survive.

Examining the strategies of C-level executives of various companies, you immediately see that some approach the markets more wisely and with more foresight than others. The same is true for whole industries. An example of an industry that has shown itself to be reluctant to take the signs of the times seriously is the automobile industry – though some companies are doing significantly better than others.

Let's take General Motors as one of many possible non-Taoist examples within that industry. GM provides a perfect illustration of a company that is relying on past models and has lost its balance. The executives, the corporate culture, the suppliers, the unions – just about every element of the complex mix had gone wrong.

The result was that GM was too slow to react to changes in the market, too slow to pick up on new trends with regard to SUVs and fuel-efficient cars, too slow to cut costs to preserve the health of the company. Detroit's long-term reluctance to recognize the trend away from fossil fuels and towards sustainable energy sources is one of the most prominent examples, but there are many more.

What does this tell us about GM's corporate culture? That it is not forward looking, that it does not embrace change, that it is arrogant and inflexible and blind to the new realities of the market.

The senior management of GM and other US auto companies, just as with Wall Street's former superstars, found it difficult to adapt to the new circumstances. The selfish and myopic greed evident in so many corporate decisions highlights the extent to which they and their industries had veered away from a Taoist path. The Taoist way is to try to avoid having to repair things and to make continuous interference in processes unnecessary.

Sticking with the automobile industry for

a moment, we can see quite a contrast between GM and Toyota, with its so-called *Toyota Way* – the source of the Western *Lean* "movement". The *Toyota Way* means to be very responsive in dealing with issues, processes and people.

Probably because of its intense focus on results, Toyota has always stressed the cooperative principle, be it between management and employees or among employees themselves. If your goal is to "eliminate waste at all levels", you have to care for your people. The Toyota culture of "continuous improvement" is coherent and fine-tuned – whether we are talking about manufacturing processes or the management of people. It is one consistent whole.

A corporate organism such as this, which is continuously adapting and absorbing knowledge, is in much better shape to spot trends and tendencies. This is why Toyota was the first automobile manufacturer reacting to widespread environmental concerns. It launched the Prius, the first mass-produced hybrid car worldwide, in 1997.

In 2006, Toyota was the first non-American

company ever to make it into the top ten of *Fortune Magazine*'s "America's Most Admired Companies", and with good reason. But even an efficient and receptive management culture is not immune to disruptions. This became apparent with Toyota's expansion outside Japan. Corporate growth did not occur organically, but was promoted all too actively – and a certain complacency set in.

Fujio Cho, then President of Toyota, was very well aware of this. At a 2004 management conference in Traverse City, USA, he gave a speech entitled "Re-inventing Toyota." He talked about "a sense of crisis at Toyota" and the need to be constantly recreating the company. Some people might have regarded this as a bizarre exaggeration – Toyota was the world's most profitable automobile manufacturer at that time. But if a proactive attitude is not deeply embedded into the corporate culture, a company might pay dearly for it.

Many people assume the *Daodejing* to be promoting passivity. This simply is a misinterpretation. Instead, the *Daodejing* is one of the early proponents of a very proactive approach to affairs. It strongly advocates being farsighted in one's actions in order to reduce the time and effort you might otherwise have to invest in solving preventable problems. Quite simply, this is time and effort which would be better spent on more constructive activities.

A prudent and farsighted approach to dealings and investments is something that definitely characterizes the management style of Li Ka-shing, chairman of Cheung Kong Ltd and Hutchinson Whampoa Ltd, whose head office is in Hong Kong. This is, without any doubt, one of the main reasons for his being able to change from being a have-not to presiding over an empire of more than 200,000 employees spread over 52 countries.

Preventing trouble by focusing on details and especially on weak spots, occupies a prominent role in his thoughts on management. In the Q&A session after a lecture on the art of management at Shantou University in Guangdong province, China, he gave the following quote from chapter 44 of the *Daodejing*: "If you know when to stop, you will not get into danger."

Chapter 63 says: "When you plan diffi-cult things, focus on what is simple in them. When you want to accomplish great things, pay attention to the tiny details.... This is why the sages never do big things, but can achieve great results."

A complicated layout stays complicated throughout. It is difficult to execute and dif-ficult to communicate. Instead, make things easily accessible. Complexity can be good, but complicatedness is always bad.

Think of crystals. Their complexity comes through an endless multiplication of a simple structure. When you analyse an operational pattern from a Taoist point of view, you will ask: What will be the effect on a macro level, if you endlessly multiply that pattern?

Do things in simple steps. This makes the process of accomplishing difficult tasks easier, safer and more stable.

To some extent, the *Daodejing*'s advice is simply about careful planning and strategic management. Its real emphasis, however, is on truly efficient, agile and responsive operational patterns. You can do a lot of planning, but if your everyday operational patterns are inefficient, you are wasting precious resources.

Wuwei has an important share in this. It is about avoiding the necessity of interference, making processes as clean and as effective as possible. The more you interfere in processes, the more you have to deal with their some-times obvious, but often unpredictable and latent effects. Approaching things with a *wu-wei* attitude, you will first of all avoid or at least minimize friction, and second you will become aware of and settle problems at a stage when they are still easy to manage.

In this respect, it is highly significant for a business to select the right people. Professional competence is not enough. It is equally important to have a high awareness of one's own personal strengths and weaknesses, and the ability to admit weaknesses and to communicate ideas and problems openly and directly.

The better that communication and ef-fective communication channels have been established in your business, the sooner you will learn about issues that might become problems, and the sooner you can fix them. Besides good products and services, effective communication structures within your company can provide you with a definite competitive advantage.

Revenue figures are of course important. But they do not necessarily give you an accurate and balanced account of the health of your business. You can generate high annual revenues but nevertheless do badly relative to the potential of your business. Underutilizing the available potential of a company or situation only leads to waste and problems.

A venture often gets quite a lot of attention when being launched. But in the course of time, slackness sneaks in. However, it is often the little, seemingly insignificant, details that are neglected for too long that cause serious trouble. As it says in the *Daodejing*: "Be as careful at the end as you are at the beginning, and there will be no unsuccessful matters." (Chapter 64)

Sometimes it is your own decisions and

actions that later force you to radically change course. Read what the *Daodejing* has to say: "What you desire to reduce, must first have been expanded. What you desire to weaken, must first have been strengthened. What you desire to destroy, must first have been established. What you desire to seize, must first have been relinquished." (Chapter 36)

There are always many factors over which you have little or no control. But many complications and problems can be avoided if you ensure that the operating procedures in your business are efficient and intelligent on all levels.

Everything you do causes a chain of reactions. Every single action has a range of side effects. Make them work for and not against you.

Chapter 3

Competing in the Marketplace

Tao Takeaways

-  Maximize positive side effects
- Remember that a good warrior is not hot-tempered
- Hone your soft skills
- Be flexible
- Fix things before they turn into real problems

生 而 不 有
为 而 不 恃
长 而 不 宰

Create, but do not be possessive.

Chapter 4
Being The Boss

Lead, but do not rule

"Bring forth, but do not be possessive; act, but do not be presumptuous; lead, but do not rule." (Daodejing, chapter 51)

"Leading, but not ruling": that is the operational mode of the Tao. This is also the style of leadership Taoist sage leaders adopt for themselves. To guide rather than to insist. To influence rather than order. A cooperative approach to leadership motivates and inspires people. Barack Obama, for example, gives every indication of walking on a Taoist path in this regard, whether he knows it or not.

If, on the other hand, you see yourself as the lone wolf, the king of the hill, leading people in an autocratic fashion, then you should be clear that by doing so, you are wasting a lot of resources and potential. If you are that kind of leader, people will be less likely to be frank with you for fear that openness will backfire on them. By not listening to others, by insisting that things be done your way, you overlook the potential of diversity, and lose the opportunity to benefit from the creativity and enthusiasm of your staff and your customers. Such behavior is detrimental to the health of your business.

Anne Mulcahy, CEO (until July 2009) and chairwoman of Xerox, provides a perfect illustration of the value of listening well. When, in 2000, she was appointed president, Xerox was in deep trouble, with revenues declining at a double digit rate and debts of $18 billion. It was very close to bankruptcy.

As she recounts in a talk she gave at Stanford Graduate School of Business in 2004, she spent the first three months travelling, listening to and speaking with everybody who could tell her something about Xerox's problems – employees, customers, industry experts. She calls herself a Chief Communications Officer. Apart from all other talents and professional skills, it was this ability and eagerness to listen and openly communicate that enabled Mulcahy to effectively address the problems and get Xerox back on track.

It does not matter whether the organizational structure of your company is hierarchical or flat. Even in very hierarchical structures, there is no need for managers to act in an autocratic fashion. You are much more likely to get better results if you use a cooperative style.

You need to be aware that you are the decision maker, the most powerful person in the room, and also that it is difficult for others to speak up in the face of your power. The *Daodejing*'s advice is for you, the dominant individual in a situation. Its advice is basically is downplay that power. Real strength has no need to show off.

A cooperative style of leadership always empowers people. Most people possess much more potential than their everyday life allows or motivates them to display. In uninspiring situations, people only make very limited use of their potential. If you can create an atmosphere of confidence and enthusiasm at and about work, in other words a workplace that is meaningful for staff, you will have naturally hardworking employees. Ask yourself how much confidence and enthusiasm you sense when you come to the office in the morning. Take this reality check next time you get there.

Empowerment happens on a number of different levels. It can mean that you delegate more and better, giving people more freedom of action as well as more responsibility – more freedom to create solutions and make decisions, more responsibility for the results. Delegating better means endeavoring to understand your staff and their potential and helping them grow as they perform their tasks.

Besides allowing for and encouraging more participation on an organizational level, empowerment also means more space for personal development. People who can see that there are real opportunities in their company to develop professionally and personally every day are highly motivated and productive. If you are able to create such an environment, to provide the resources needed and to gather together a team of people that is professionally and emotionally competent, you can "conquer the world".

Richard Branson, chairman of the Virgin Group, is a conqueror of this kind – and demonstrates the unconventional side of wisdom. According to its website, Virgin has created more than 200 companies worldwide and employs approximately 50,000 people in 29 countries. As Branson explained in a TED interview in 2007, Virgin's success is all about "finding the right people, inspiring them and drawing out the best in them". He is doing this in a very empowering way, taking care to ensure that people love their jobs.

Success is of course not tied to a specific style of leadership. There are many examples of successful CEOs known for their cooperative style of leadership as well as examples of successful autocratic CEOs. The question is how do you define success? Success in terms of numbers is important from a Taoist perspective too, but it is not measured by high-climbing revenues and rising stock prices alone. Leaders who are called successful from a Taoist point of view, ensure the long-term viability of their organization. They also see beyond the affairs of daily business and view profitability within a larger societal and global context.

Your ability to choose staff wisely and work with them effectively is reflected partly through the level of staff turnover in your company. Low staff turnover shows your competence as a boss.

Being proficient in this area can allow you to make huge savings. Dissatisfied employees cost money. They ask for sick leave more often and are less efficient in their own work. They de-energize other staff members and diminish the productivity of the whole team, and they are more likely to resign, leaving you with the expense of finding and training a replacement.

Autocratic leaders are proud of having the power to decide matters of "life and death" for their people. But it is definitely not a sign of personal strength, if someone needs to be feared in order to be able to govern. Good leaders are not focused on themselves; they focus on the people they lead.

The *Daodejing* names four types of leaders and the different effects they have on people:

"The greatest leaders are those who people below only know of as being there. They are followed by the ones who people want to get close to and praise. Then there are those who are feared. They are followed by those who are despised … The greatest leaders complete their tasks and settle their agendas, and yet the people will say: 'We are what we are on our own accord.'" (Chapter 17)

Non-action and no agenda

"Act without taking action, and there is nothing that cannot be governed." (*Daodejing*, chapter 3)

As I have said before, to depict the *Daodejing* as promoting passivity is a misinterpretation. You cannot govern a country or lead a company by doing nothing. The whole *Daodejing* is about the art of leadership. It is about action. But the *Daodejing* does emphasize modes of action that are non-manipulative and noninterfering, actions that are beneficial to society, to the environment and to yourself.

Wuwei is about effortlessness. It is about hitting the bull's-eye every time. This requires true awareness of yourself and others. This requires work, and action of some sort.

First of all, you might have to make improvements to certain parts of your personality. Personal development is the key factor for achieving *wuwei*. A person who regularly overrules his or her inner voice and intuition is a far way from acting in a *wuwei* mode. The more you ignore or oppose parts of yourself, the more opposition and friction you will meet in the outside world.

People are motivated and inspired by charisma, but they also react to every inconsistency in a boss's behavior. This can significantly reduce the performance of your employees. If you want to be the kind of boss that gets the best results from your people, your actions should be consistent with your words, thoughts and emotions.

To optimize the ratio between input and output, you have to take care that your input of time, energy, money and resources gets maximum results. *Wuwei* means no unnecessary attrition. It means not leaving traces caused by resistance or any kind of emotional scars.

The *Daodejing* (in chapter 27) says: "A good traveler does not leave cart tracks or foot prints. A good talker is not a target of reproach. A person who is good at calculations does not need a counting rod. A person good at closing does not need a lock to prevent something from being opened. A person good at tying knots does not need a rope to prevent something from being untied."

Try to use as little effort as possible. An example from the martial arts: When you throw a punch and you are trying too hard, it is easy to see what you are up to, which eliminates any possibility for surprise. Trying too hard also makes you more tense, which means your punches will be slower and have less impact. On the other hand, if you are operating in a *wuwei* mode, you just let it happen, you move and punch with ease. There is then less to inhibit the flow of energy and you make optimal use of your potential.

In a business context, this means: Requesting too much or using too much control makes a process more complicated than it has to be. In turn, not only additional time and energy, but also interference is needed to keep it on track or to get it back there again. But this is a waste of resources. As a boss, it is better to ensure that processes and communication in your company run smoothly from start to finish, eliminating any unnecessary attrition.

The *Daodejing* loves paradoxes. Being without an agenda in taking over the empire is just another one of those.

"The empire is always taken by being without an agenda. Having an agenda, you are not qualified to take over the empire." (*Daodejing*, chapter 48)

As with *wuwei*, non-action, *wushi*, being without an agenda, is not about having no agenda at all. It is about not having an egocentric or antisocial agenda. It is a call for social responsibility. Social responsibility, however, starts within your company, with a caring attitude towards your employees.

One thing that the *Daodejing* repeatedly emphasizes is the importance of supporting and encouraging people to unveil their potential. Here is one example: "As the sages say: I have no agendas and the people fare well by themselves. I am without action and the people develop by themselves."(Chapter 57)

As a boss you are always faced with the question of how to make the best use of human potential. You can do everything in your power to really help people unlock their potential. But if instead your actions are perceived as meddling or too demanding, you are impeding your staff's workflow and diminishing their performance.

Be a model person

"Sages reside in the affairs of non-action and practice instruction without words." (*Daodejing*, chapter 2)

What people are looking for in a leader is direction, but also support. The *Daodejing* does not stress or approve of silence. On the contrary, words and concepts are given a high degree of importance. But actions and leading by example are even more important.

A boss whose behavior is incongruent, who says something that everyone knows he does not really mean, or who says A while doing B, is conditioning his staff to adopt an attitude of not being accountable for what they do. If you are inconsistent or lacking in integrity, then it allows them to be the same. Under such circumstances, you can neither work efficiently, nor make full use of available resources.

The personal traits of a boss or a manager can make a real difference. They can have considerable impact, not only on the atmosphere of the workplace, but also on many other aspects, such as employee motivation, customer satisfaction, employee and customer loyalty and the results of business negotiations.

These are not trifling matters. This is all about money. Personal development and the desire to grow and learn are essential attributes for people in leadership positions. Sometimes, however, executives neglect the fact that the way they handle even the small things in daily life can offer profound insight regarding their true grip on the big topics and strategies.

To be a good boss, it is absolutely necessary to have confidence in yourself and to enjoy the process of making decisions. But arrogance and pretentiousness make you blind to things that can be improved. They impair your agility and stifle your ability to adapt to change.

Fujio Cho of Toyota is a good example of an unpretentious leader. To some extent, his demeanor might simply be an expression of traditional Asian modesty. But more importantly, it is a perfect expression of a long standing corporate culture and strategy that puts a strong focus on continuous learning and improvement – permeating the entire company, from the highest ranks down to the worker on the production line.

Though of all of Toyota's success, Fujio Cho has warned against complacency and resting on one's laurels. In "Full Speed Ahead", an article in *Fortune Magazine* in 2005, he gave the example of pulling a handcart up a steep hill. Losing attention for even a split second can send you down the hill again – no matter how successfully you might have taken the cart to lofty heights.

In the *Daodejing* it says: "Someone who shows off is not enlightened. Someone who is self-opinionated is not distinguished. Someone who boasts of himself is without merit. Someone who is arrogant is not eligible to be a leader." (Chapter 24)

If you can inspire people, if your employees admire your work style, your diligence, patience, ability to listen, to mediate, to motivate and support, to give direction, to stay calm under pressure, to make fast and intelligent decisions, they will definitely give their best to support you in return.

The attitude of serving

"The rivers and the sea are kings of a hundred mountain streams, because they can place themselves below them. This is why they can be kings to the hundred mountain streams. When sages are in front of people, they place themselves behind them. When they are on top of people, they are humble." (*Daodejing*, chapter 66)

The *Daodejing*'s point of view, that leaders should heed their mandate to serve the people they lead, is as relevant as ever. This is not idealism. The *Daodejing* is a pragmatic book focused on efficiency. Its advice, originally intended for political leaders, also makes good business sense.

Some people in leadership positions behave as if they were autocratic monarchs. But a few things should be clear with such bosses: besides creating an oppressive and demotivating atmosphere, their style of leadership leads them to neglect potential and resources, and lose opportunities for progress.

In the course of their careers, most people encounter different types of bosses, among them the autocratic monarch type, possibly egocentric and moody. If you have ever experienced the negative power of such an environment, you know what this means in terms of motivation, energy, creativity and performance. If, on the other hand, you have also had a boss who was supportive and committed to his people, you will remember how that boosted your motivation and the difference it made in terms of your own commitment and performance.

Maybe you are the boss. If so, if you are committed to your employees, you will see a definite return. Maybe the term "to serve" seems old-fashioned, uncool, and not compatible with the image of an alpha leader. But you will benefit from working for your staff.

Think of the service industries – retail, restaurants, hotels. Good business for such companies is a matter of service. If your service is bad, customers will not return and the word will spread. Your bad service will benefit your competitors.

If, however, you really want to provide first class service you go beyond the superficial. You need to be consistent and coherent all the way through. Aiming at good service for your customers, but at the same time neglecting your employees, will definitely not produce the desired results. The idea of perfect service has to be ingrained in every little detail of your business. Otherwise it will always simply be part of the crowd, but never really stand out and achieve excellence.

Employees are, of course, different from customers. It is not as easy for them to leave their jobs or switch to another employer as it is for a customer to walk into another shop. But if the conditions you offer your staff are unsatisfactory, the service they provide to you will likewise be unsatisfactory. At the very least, they will not go that extra mile for you. They will make you less money than they could do. This is the "win-win" concept. If you are a supportive and motivating boss, your staff will help you to make more money.

There are many passages in the *Daodejing* on leadership. I believe that this one on the Three Treasures is really sums up what a great leader is made of:

"I have three treasures that I keep and preserve. The first treasure is a caring attitude. The second treasure is being thrifty. The third treasure is being modest. Because of a caring attitude one can be courageous. Being thrifty one can be generous. Because of modesty, one can become the leader of others. Fighting with a caring attitude means winning, using it for defense means stabilizing things." (*Daodejing*, chapter 67)

Chapter 4

Being the Boss

Tao Takeaways

● Be a cooperative leader

● Be responsive, do not force things

● Never get complacent

● Value social engagement

● Support your staff

● Be a model person

善用人者为之下

A person good at managing others
places himself below them.

Chapter 5
Managing a Team

Ziran - Be natural and authentic

"Humans find orientation in earth. Earth finds orientation in Heaven. Heaven finds orientation in the Tao. The Tao finds orientation in *ziran*." (*Daodejing*, chapter 25)

Ziran is a concept that is difficult to translate into a single English word. As with *wuwei*, I use the Chinese transcription rather than confining it to the straightjacket of any one English word, thereby leaving more space for understanding its full meaning.

The above quote from chapter 25 is an important statement in the *Daodejing*, since it is the Tao that later gave Taoism and Taoists their name. The reason why *ziran* is a concept of such significance in the *Daodejing* is because it describes a central feature of the Tao.

Ziran literally translates as to be "like that of one's own accord". What this means is being natural, being authentic, basically being in harmony with and going along with the potential within oneself.

Ziran is the foundation of *wuwei*, non-action, and the prerequisite for going with the flow. If you are *ziran*, you are in balance. A person who is not balanced needs to constantly rely on interference to get things back on track. Corrective interference, however, is much less efficient than amplifying existing potential.

Ziran is an extremely valuable tool in communication, both with yourself and with others. If your communication with yourself is unimpeded and free flowing, you have the best possible foundation for comprehensive communication with others. People who regularly overrule their inner voices are hardly open and responsive enough to process all the information that can be received consciously and subconsciously from others. The more information you are able to absorb and process, the more you can read between the lines of a situation, and the more options you have to optimize communication within your team.

Improving communication with yourself has direct positive effects on your rapport with your team.

Sometimes, people do not tell you straight out what is on their minds or what is really going on in a situation. What they tell you is only half the story. But more often than not, as long as your intuition and instinctive antennae are working well, you can spot the situations where you are getting only half the story. Making good use of all your instincts and capacities offers you the opportunity to address issues at an early stage, making it much easier to ensure that processes run as smoothly as possible from start to finish.

When there are difficulties in communication, no matter whether they are new ones or whether they have already existed for a while, sometimes even minimal changes can either complicate or dissolve tension and discontent. The more you, as the team leader, are in touch with yourself and emotionally balanced, the more easily you can avoid and resolve problems and get things back on a smooth track.

You do not only communicate with words.

Watch your reactions. Try to send positive and encouraging signals. The degree to which you succeed in doing this mainly depends on how balanced you are as a person. Balance radiates, and provides a solid basis for effective leadership.

As a boss, you set the rules of the game. When staff see that you are someone who is thinking what you say, saying what you think and doing what you say, you encourage them to be the same.

In the Taoists emulating the Tao, *ziran* plays a key role. *Ziran* is important for leaders, but it is also something they want to foster in the people lead by them. The *Daodejing* says: "This is why sages … are able to support *ziran* in all beings and do not dare to act." (Chapter 64)

Mentoring and coaching is important in every environment. But it is especially important for Western businesses in economies like the Chinese one where you are commonly faced with high staff turnover rates. Here it is significant as a means to attract talent to your company and keep it there.

A team that operates in a *ziran* mode is easier to lead and works more efficiently. All processes within a company relate to communication. Optimizing communication, and fostering an atmosphere of enthusiasm and openness in your business are important factors in terms of guaranteeing your own success.

Be adaptive

"A person who takes action on something, destroys it. A person who holds on to something loses it. This is why sages do not act, so nothing is ruined. They do not hold on to anything, so nothing is lost." (*Daodejing*, chapter 64)

The *Daodejing*'s concept of *wuzhi*, "not holding on", is closely related to *wuwei* and *ziran*. Analogous to *wuwei*, "not holding on" does not mean you should not hold on to anything. This is seen in chapter 35: "When you hold on to the big image [the Tao], the world will come to you." It would be impossible to do absolutely nothing and hold on to absolutely nothing. The meaning of "not holding on" is to not hold onto something inflexibly.

To avoid any misunderstanding: too long can sometimes refer to just a split second of inattention.

Take whitewater kayaking, for example. When you get into difficult rapids or have to handle steep drops, you need to be highly adaptive and in tune with yourself. In a situation where there is no time to think about anything twice, tiny mistakes can have huge effects.

Not holding on requires a high level of flexibility and the ability to adapt quickly to changing situations and challenges. How do you foster this ability? It calls for awareness and continuous cultivation. Do not take anything for granted. The only thing that is certain is that things change, sometimes slowly, sometimes quickly.

As I just mentioned above, not holding on is closely related to *ziran*. A person who is not well balanced, who is not in tune with his or her capabilities has to hold on to many more things than someone who is balanced.

This is why balance within a team is so

important for productivity and efficiency. Balance can be approached on different levels. What I am talking about here is not a surface level. Something looking fine from the outside does not mean that on other levels there is balance as well. An important factor in building a balanced team is who is chosen to become a member of the team. An at least equally important factor is the personality of its leader. To get the best results from teams, their leaders need to have professional skills, just as they need to have balance and emotional intelligence.

This is why personal development is so significant. For someone in a leading position, *holding on* drastically reduces the ability to take quick action in a crisis. Personal development never stops, it is a lifelong process. To be as flexible as possible, you need to be open and relaxed, and possess confidence in your senses and instincts and make full use of them. Only then is your way open to spontaneous and fast action / "non-action".

Different people address tasks in different ways. A boss who insists on his or her way without checking on the opinion of others first is not making effective use of the diversity and experience of the whole team. The result, inevitably, is that productivity suffers. But if you offer support and encouragement and provide a platform where all members of the team have a chance to make use of their individual abilities and talents, then diversity is working for you.

To do this, you need to be able to tune in to what is going on around you.

There are many factors that influence communication within a team. It is important in all kinds of contexts not to hold on to things too tightly. Don't be too categorical in stating your opinions in meetings with your staff. Always leave open the possibility for other points of view to be expressed. This is very helpful in terms of team interaction. Manage all situations involving the potential for conflict or confrontation in a way that is positive, open and productive. The precondition for creativity is the free flow of energy. Tension and a dictatorial style impede it.

Emotional intelligence

"Someone who is good at employing people places himself below them. This is called the *De* of non-competition. This is called making use of other people's strengths." (*Daodejing*, chapter 68)

The *Dao* (Tao) and the *De* of the *Daodejing* belong together. Despite all the *Daodejing* has to say about it, Tao (*Dao*) is a word which ultimately defies precise description. *De*, however, stands for the concrete realization of the *Dao*. It is a word commonly translated as "virtue". As I did with *ziran*, I use the transliteration *De* to avoid too narrow an interpretation. Many of the concepts in the *Daodejing* are like mathematical variables, which makes them extremely functional. You have to look at them in concrete situations to be able to ascribe specific meanings to them.

Handling emotions is an issue underestimated by many people in business. But as studies by Daniel Goleman and others clearly show, emotional intelligence is quiet significant for successful leadership.

Emotional competence is in high demand, especially in situations that are strongly governed by emotions – such as conflict, distinct disagreement and dissatisfaction. The more responsive leaders are, the faster they can deal with an issue at hand and settle it.

The *Daodejing* has much to say about the psychology of leadership.

The passage quoted above is very much about motivation. Its frame of mind is this: When people see that their leaders are acting in their best interests, there will be a reciprocal effect. This is a typical "win-win" mindset. To get maximum cooperation from your team, you need to give them clear opportunities to benefit. Truly cooperative behavior within a team, meaning full commitment, only occurs when the boss creates a truly cooperative environment.

Herb Kelleher, former CEO of Southwest Airlines, represents an attitude that is very much in line with the *Daodejing*'s view of the relationship between leaders and the people for whom they are responsible. Kelleher created a positive, inspiring and caring atmosphere for the staff of Southwest, and saw them as the first customers for him to take care of. This created for the staff an extremely strong sense of identification with the company. To maintain this culture, Kelleher paid tremendous attention to the hiring process, looking for people with a "predisposition to serve others", instead of hiring people who were self-centred, as he explained in a 2007 interview for *LeaderNetwork*.

A topic addressed in chapter 17 of the *Daodejing*, and discussed in chapter 2 of this book, is trust. Not showing enough trust and confidence in employees is demotivating and undermines the self-confidence of staff. At the same time, it also reveals a manager's lack of self-confidence.

A boss with low emotional competencies produces a lot of "waste", thereby drastically reducing output. This is bad use of the potential within the team.

Managing teams successfully requires good communication skills and high emotional intelligence, both of which can be learned. A good boss is able to handle all kinds of personalities and can get the best results from different types of people.

In referring to the best type of leaders, the *Daodejing* says: "They are cautious and pay great attention to their words." (Chapter 17)

It is often less *what* you say than *how* you say it that makes the difference. This especially holds true when passing on criticism when things are not running smoothly. If you want an employee to make improvements in work performance, your words, your facial expressions and gestures can either motivate or demotivate. As a boss, it makes no business sense to sap your employees' energy.

A nice story in the *Zhuangzi* goes like this: "The master of the monkeys gave them chestnuts saying: 'You will have three scoops in the morning and four in the evening.' The monkeys were very displeased. So he said, 'Alright, then you can have four scoops in the morning and three in the evening.' And the monkeys were happy. The hard facts stayed the same, but the different arrangement resulted in either delight or displeasure."

(Chapter 2)

Another example of how a situation can be affected by what you say and when and how you say it, is when an employer considers firing a staff member.

From a Taoist point of view, firing people should always be the last step in seeking a solution to a problem. It is worth remembering that termination of an employee does not take place in a vacuum. The way you implement it is emblematic of your corporate culture. The basic Taoist attitude to consider here is expressed in chapter 27 of the *Daodejing*: "Sages are always good at assisting people. They do not abandon people."

When you observe employees underperforming or creating problems, talk with them, their colleagues and superiors about the specific issues as soon as you become aware of them. You want to give the company and the people within it the opportunity to learn and to improve. If, however, various methods do not resolve a problem and you have good reason to ask somebody to leave, do it in a respectful, frank and honest way. Sometimes it is better for an employee to find another job and career direction and for the company to find a more suitable replacement.

If you handle the termination well, it will have a positive effect on the rest of the team. If you do it poorly, the impact on the team will be negative. Always aim to do more good than harm.

Consistency and continuity

"A person standing on tiptoe cannot really stand well. A person making big strides cannot take long walks. A person who shows off does not shine. A person who is self-opinionated is not distinguished. A person who boasts is without merit. A person who is arrogant is ineligible to be a leader." (*Daodejing*, chapter 24)

This quote, about how standing on tiptoes and striding cannot provide consistent performance, comes from a chapter which talks about how negative personal traits disqualify a leader, or at least distinguish a bad one from a good one. The ideal leader is characterized in another chapter in the following way:

"Sages are a model for the world. They do not show off, therefore they shine. They are not self-opinionated, therefore they are distinguished. They do not boast of themselves, therefore they have merit. They are not arrogant, therefore they are leaders. Because they do not compete, nobody in the world is able to compete with them." (*Daodejing*, chapter 22)

The personality traits of a leader have a significant influence on the behavior and performance of the subordinates. Ideal leaders do not need to show off, nor do they need to play the Big Boss, because aside from professional competence, they possess what you might call real strength. They are emotionally well balanced. On an intellectual as well as on an emotional level, they avoid provoking opposition and conscious or subconscious sabotage from staff.

A boss whose words and actions are not consistent sends conflicting signals creating a whole range of negative side effects. If you want continuity in the productivity and efficiency of your team, you have to be consistent in your directives and promises.

When you ask your team to stretch, you must be aware that this is only going to work for a limited period of time. When people see that you do not ask too much of them, or that you ask as much of yourself as you do of them, then they will do their best to match or exceed your expectations.

While looking for consistent quality and productivity in your team, be careful not to be unrealistic in your assignments and expectations. Setting unrealistic goals is counterproductive. When people do their best, but meet with disapproval for not being good enough, they get frustrated and their productivity declines. Intelligent encouragement, however, is a powerful tool to keep up motivation and levels of continuously high productivity. Encourage responsiveness in your team to guarantee consistency of your team's performance.

It is natural for people to want to perform well. If you are consistent in your actions, if you are really supportive and motivating, offering long-term perspectives and incentives to your employees, you will create an environment that encourages this natural tendency to come to full bloom.

Chapter 5

Managing a Team

Tao Takeaways

- Amplify existing potential
- Stay open
- Watch your emotional competencies
- Be consistent

是以能辅万物之
自然而弗敢为

Sages know how to support
the natural potential in all things.

Chapter 6

Creating Workplaces

Company facilities and efficiency

The previous two chapters were mainly concerned with general strategies to improve performance and factors which increase or decrease employee motivation, productivity and efficiency – always with a strong emphasis on workplace atmosphere.

Something I have not talked about so far is the actual work space. Being the material environment in which you and your staff spend your days, office spaces and other company facilities play an essential role in motivation, productivity and efficiency. They either assist or prevent energies from flowing.

Functionality of office space is often considered in terms of fitting as many people as possible into as small a space as possible in order to save on rental costs. But rather than focusing too much on saving money and calculating how much or little floor space each employee can put up with, you might want to think in more constructive terms of what would be most likely to create a communication-friendly, motivating and productive environment for the kind of work involved, and have your office or office building designed accordingly. The simple reason for this is that happy and motivated employees make more money for your company than do unhappy and demotivated employees.

Feng Shui

Western surveys underline the importance of office design for job engagement and pro-ductivity. This is of no surprise to anyone acquainted with Feng Shui. Feng Shui is an ancient Chinese tradition dating from far antiquity and based on collected human ex-perience over many millennia. There is a lot of hocus pocus associated with it these days, as you can easily see from a browse through the Feng Shui books on the shelf of any major bookstore. But real Chinese Feng Shui is profound and there are good reasons why it has survived through the ages.

Its main aim is to ensure that architectural layout and arrangements are conducive to a harmonious, healthy and prosperous life. There is much to learn in the field of Feng Shui. It is a lot more than a matter of randomly rearranging a few pieces of furniture, adding a bit of color here or there, or hanging a mirror to drive away evil spirits. Nor is Feng Shui purely a matter of design. Spaces can be beautifully designed but completely impractical or contain an atmosphere that stunts inspiration. Feng Shui is about arranging our environment in a way that preserves and enhances harmony, health and wealth.

Whether you believe in Feng Shui or not, one thing can be said with certainty. The way in which rooms and buildings are designed and arranged has a tremendous influence on how we feel, on how motivated, and eventually on how productive we are.

A life in the office

We only have to think of the huge amount of time people spend in the office. For many people, their office becomes almost a second home. But spending a great deal of your time at the office is no guarantee for productivity and efficiency.

Many people actually spend more time at the office than they do at home, reducing the amount of time available for themselves and for their families. So it makes sense to ensure that the workplace does not leave the after-taste of being a time thief. If that is the impression that a work environment leaves on staff, then you can be sure that they will not be as motivated as they could be. Nor will you.

A smart Taoist company creates office spaces in which everyone enjoys spending time.

You can take aspects of private life and make them part of office life. You can create spaces that allow for communication and relaxation, something more than a dull coffee and tea corner; areas where you can talk to your colleagues and exchange thoughts, and also quiet areas to recharge your batteries, where people can have a brain break. For people spending most of the day in front of a computer screen, to stay focused and productive sometimes only requires the occasional short break. Often ideas flow much better after such short breaks. And this happens more easily in comfortable spaces.

Natural connectors

People who have a window in their office which gives them a view of nature know how energizing this can be. But even if you are not so privileged, and work in an office space in a large building in a big city with skyscrapers all around, possibly without any window at all, you can still make use of the power of nature. You can integrate natural elements like water, wood or plants into your work environment, instead of being completely surrounded by synthetic materials. Natural elements are very powerful in terms of restoring energy levels. Make intelligent use of them in your office and company facilities.

If you are successful and you want to stay successful or become even more so in the future, then tap into the potential that you and your employees possess, and make better use of it. To go with the flow, you need to be in tune with yourself. You need to have a good feeling for yourself and for the rhythm of your surroundings. Office spaces can help or hinder you in this. If you want more engagement and input from your employees, it makes good business sense to plan offices with maximum employee comfort and productivity in mind.

Chapter 6

Creating Workplaces

Tao Takeaways

- 🌓 Create facilities that increase motivation

- 🌓 Build offices that assist energies to flow

- 🌓 Plan spaces with maximum comfort and productivity in mind

静为躁君

Tranquility governs haste.

Chapter 7
Dealing with Stress

Caring for life

Under stress, people tend to offset their frustrations with habits such as drinking too much coffee or alcohol, or developing strong cravings for sweets and junk food.

Such actions do not reduce stress, nor do they increase efficiency. Instead, they eventually undermine a person's physical and emotional health. This relates to the *Daodejing*'s emphasis on natural things without "artificial" flavoring or embellishment, and on the importance of working to reduce cravings and desires.

It makes more sense to do things that help you to stay physically fit, to become more emotionally balanced and stable and to train yourself to live in tune with the calm rhythms inside you.

Tranquility

"Heaviness is the root of lightness. Tranquility governs haste." (*Daodejing*, chapter 26)

In order to effectively cope with stress, and the loss of concentration, hasty decision making and irritableness that usually accompanies it, you had better make sure that stress does not take hold of you. You need to always have a nucleus of calmness and tranquility within yourself. To continuously cultivate this nucleus of peace is of great value. It is a resource that enables you to tap into potential and creativity deep within yourself and to keep your mind clear and focused.

Muddy water constantly in motion cannot settle.

An important guideline for Chinese martial arts as well as for meditation, calligraphy, music and painting is this: "There is tranquility within movement and movement within tranquility."

Most people in the West immediately think of jumping kicks or other acrobatic highlights, and not of tranquility, when they think of Chinese martial arts. But it is surely not because of the flashy parts of martial arts are held in such high esteem in Chinese culture. It is their profound medical, philosophical and strategic side which has earned them the reputation of being a cultural treasure.

You might have heard of the Chinese martial art called Tai Chi. You have probably seen people doing it. The slow and graceful movements of Tai Chi are a good example of "tranquility within movement". These movements tune the body, soothe and strengthen both body and mind. Just watching Tai Chi can give you a sense of calmness.

But "tranquility within movement" is also a guideline for fast and dynamic Chinese martial arts styles. Fast does not mean hectic. In order to be fully balanced and strong, movements need to revolve around a center that is calm and tranquil. They need to have a good rhythm. This rhythm cannot be fixed by anyone but you. It is something you have to find within yourself.

These ideas are certainly not limited to Chinese martial arts. But through their training routines you can learn a good deal about your strengths and weaknesses and get inspiration and valuable suggestions for the way you approach tasks in professional life.

When you are looking for consistency and continuity even under stress, your activities have to be conducted in calmness. Anything you can do that calms you and helps you to put aside your worries is precious.

People who stay calm even when engaged in difficult tasks requiring speed, concentration and coordination have charisma. They have a significant impact on other people.

If you are able to stay calm and attuned with your own rhythm, no matter what you are doing, you do not have to worry about stress. You will sense when you are crossing the line, and proactively take steps to offset the stress before it becomes too much.

To understand the opposite concept of "movement within tranquility", think of meditation.

When you sit still in meditation, everything inside of you becomes calm and on the exterior you appear to be hardly moving. But you are still working on the movement of your breathing. With your deep, fine breathing you send almost invisible ripples through your whole body which gradually connect every part with all other parts, providing you with a completely new sense of unity.

From the perspective of an outside observer, you are just sitting and doing nothing. But in reality, there is a lot going on inside you.

Meditation helps to make you more emotionally balanced and opens up your mind. It offers far more than simple stress relief. It can reveal a fascinating path of lifelong learning and personal development.

Efficiently dealing with stress is an important issue for everyone. It is essential for anyone in a top position with significant responsibilities to have their stress levels under control. Crucial decisions affecting many people may depend upon it.

Stress takes a significant toll on both the body and on the mind, and it is important to regularly recharge your batteries so that you are able to maintain the energy levels you need to operate effectively as a leader. Schedule periods of calm into your daily routine to help you to contain stress. It could be as simple as going for a walk, or gazing out of the window for a few minutes.

The point to absorb is that when you become agitated, reason and intuition are easily overruled. Both agitated behavior and calmness are contagious. A team led by a boss who stays calm and relaxed under stress is more likely to perform well.

Can you answer the following questions posed by the *Daodejing* in the affirmative, by saying "Me"?

"Who is able to make something that is turbulent gradually clear again through tranquility? Who is able to gradually awaken something that is still to life through long enduring motion?" (Chapter 15)

Emptiness

"Clay is made into vessels. But it is through the emptiness (in its center) that the vessel has a function … what exists is useful, what does not exist provides function." (*Daodejing*, chapter 11)

People usually focus on what exists rather than on what does not exist. The *Daodejing*, however, places strong emphasis on the functions of emptiness and nonexistence – something you should have in mind when pondering over the concepts of *wuwei* and reduction.

In Taoism, stillness and emptiness are closely linked to the practice of meditation. Even on a beginner level of meditation, you can experience its incredible strength.

The concepts of emptiness and nonexistence are very much a part of the Chinese martial arts, too. In a fight, if you provide your opponent with a target, then it will certainly be attacked. The aim of many schools of Chinese martial arts is to be "nonexistent", to deflect attacks by using as little of one's own energy as possible. Instead of working with resistance, as is done in so-called hard styles by powerfully blocking attacks, in soft styles, like in Tai Chi, you focus on evaporating, like water or air, when your opponent tries to get control of you.

The same holds true for stress. Stress needs a target. Do not provide it with one. A free and empty mind is much more difficult to attack than one that is fettered.

A manager, above all else, has to be skilled in stress management. That is the most basic element of the job description. Outstanding managers are not only good at dealing with their own stress, they can recognize and correct stress in their teams as well. This is a very valuable talent, because unstressed people work better.

In chapter 45 of the *Daodejing* it says: "Great fullness is like emptiness. Its function cannot be exhausted."

This is true for the mind as well. From a Taoist point of view, it is important to create open spaces within oneself and to explore one's inner landscapes. The mind has to be open and free. It has to be empty in order to ensure its efficiency and to be able to constantly absorb and process new information. When there are too many things on your mind, which can easily happen when you are stressed, you can lose your way. An empty mind allows you to be more receptive to new ideas, solutions and suggestions.

When you fail to deal effectively with stress, your capacity for absorbing and processing information is much reduced. But when your cup is empty, you can pour anything into it.

There is another quote from the *Daodejing* along the same lines: "The space between Heaven and Earth is like a bellows. It is empty, but it cannot be exhausted. The more it moves, the more comes out." (Chapter 5)

Focus your Ch'i and attain softness

"In concentrating Ch'i and attaining softness, can you become like an infant?" (*Daodejing*, chapter 10)

In the *Daodejing*, infants are seen as the epitome of harmony with nature, being completely in tune with the flow. They are absolutely authentic and natural, acting fully out of the needs of the situation. This is *ziran* in perfection. There is nothing artificial about them. It is all *wuwei*.

Most people fall out of this flow and continuum experience as they grow up – some earlier, some later. But if you are out of that natural balance, everything you do will be less efficient and more energy consuming. And, most important in this context, you will become stressed much more easily.

The single most effective approach to countering stress is a healthy life style, including a balanced diet, regular exercise, a harmonious family and inspiring social life, enriching hobbies and a fulfilling sex life. The lack of any one of these will make you more vulnerable to stress.

When you find yourself under considerable stress, you need something that might appear to be in very short supply: time. This is a matter of time management. You need time out, time for yourself to do things that help you to keep agile and to restore your energy levels.

Taking a spa is a wonderful way for everyone to releave stress, but especially for busy people living in cities with reduced access to nature.

Every high-end spa has a variety of select treatments and formats, and you can pick the ones that are most suitable to you. Make spa visits a part of your monthly schedule. Once in a while, spend a few days in a spa resort somewhere in a beautiful natural setting, in the mountains or next to the ocean.

Observe how fresh and reassured you feel afterwards. A spa visit can be much more than an enjoyable experience. Note the difference in your energy levels and emotional condition before and after treatment. The bigger the difference between before and after, the less efficient use you are making in your daily life of your energy potential. If you are able to maintain consistent levels of energy, you will be less vulnerable to stress. It is difficult to guarantee consistent performance if there are frequent fluctuations in your energy levels.

A powerful combination for countering stress is regular spa treatments plus regular exercise. You can jog, swim, practice Tai Chi, Yoga or meditation, make music, dance … simply do whatever you feel is good for you – but make sure you do it on a regular basis.

Even for people at the apex of their abilities, it is advisable to handle one's energy with care, to conserve it. Always be aware of the fact that your energy is finite in quantity, and while expending energy on a short-term basis, keep in mind the long-term consequences.

It is essential to foster the right attitude towards work – engaged with it but not controlled by it – and to create a workplace environment that reduces stress as much as possible. You will be confronted with stress in any highly competitive business environment. In the workplace, retain the flexibility and vigor that is so obvious in infants.

Infants are full of potential waiting to be realized. They are brimming with Ch'i and fully equipped to deal with everything awaiting them. This is the mental state that Taoists want to recapture.

Get inspiration from the spontaneity, curiosity, perseverance, enthusiasm, openness, flexibility and energy of infants.

Chapter 7

Dealing with Stress

Tao Takeaways

- Stay calm and find ways to enter tranquility

- Take things the way they are, do not let them control you

- Work with "emptiness"

- Stay agile, curious and open – learn from infants

勇于敢则杀

If you are brave in taking risks,
you will be killed.

Chapter 8

The Tao and the Global Economic Crisis

Cautiousness

Economic crises commonly do not happen out of the blue. Usually they slowly build, evolving out of a complex mix of political, economic and social factors. This is the case with the current crisis. Though there were diverse voices warning about the impending bursting of the bubble years before it happened, they were not widely given careful public consideration. The *Daodejing* says in chapter 69: "There is no bigger disaster than to underestimate one's enemy."

When we take a look at executive behavior as well as the corporate strategies of the big banks and large companies that stumbled and in some cases have already died in the current economic crisis, we discover a whole bundle of unhealthy factors. Risk evaluation models were out of whack with reality, too much confidence was placed in risky strategies and too much focus on short-term profits. The perspective on long-range economic trends was unrealistic; bonus systems did not adequately reward commitment to long-term-performance. There was arrogance, ignorance, self-deception and a lack of integrity.

However complex the reasons for the plight of companies such as Lehmann Brothers, Merrill Lynch, Fannie Mae, Freddie Mac or AIG, one thing that is both obvious and amazing at the same time is their lack of (true) awareness of risk – in spite of, or maybe because of, all their sophisticated technology and financial experts. The chief executives of these companies were in obvious contrast to the leaders praised in the *Daodejing* for following the Tao and being as "cautious as if crossing a river during winter" (chapter 15).

In chapter 73 the *Daodejing* says: "If you are brave in taking risks, you will be killed. If you are brave in not taking risks, you will live."

The fall of these companies argues for less reliance on self-assured probability models and the use of more cautious strategies. It certainly adds weight to Nassim Taleb's relentless criticism of risk management tools and the trust placed in them, particularly within the banking system.

Simple truths

Every company wants to be successful. But interactions between internal and external processes and structures have their own "natural" speed and rhythm. Artificially trying to speed up a process out of greed is detrimental to the overall health of a business.

The *Daodejing*'s advice for building something big is to be sensitive and watchful, to allow things to grow "organically" and to take mindful, small steps: "The really big matters in the world all have to arise out of minute detail." (Chapter 63)

Taoist leaders know that the shortcuts to success more often than not lead to failure, if not ruin. In chapter 53 the *Daodejing* says: "If I am endowed with some knowledge, the only thing that I am really afraid of when walking on a big road is going astray. The big road is good to walk on, but people nevertheless still like to take the shortcuts."

The current economic crisis has a massively negative impact on businesses and individuals around the world. Large numbers of people have lost their jobs, families and social networks have suffered and companies went bankrupt, all of which has had disastrous effects upon employees, local communities, the state, suppliers and creditors.

But, as it is with everything in the world, where there is something negative, there is also something positive. The crisis offers a great opportunity to wipe away a certain amount of malpractice, inefficiency and bad management. It also might clean up industries and artificially inflated economic sectors, like a fire clears the dead vegetation from a forest.

Companies that really are in touch with long-term and wide-range trends and developments, that reflect upon them and tackle them effectively, are better prepared to ride out the storm.

The crisis offers us the opportunity to heighten our awareness in many respects and on many levels. It also affirms the significance of the Taoist message for modern business: Adopt a holistic approach to strategy. The *Daodejing's* advice sometimes sounds self-evident and banal. But the most basic and simple things are often the most important and most difficult to stick to in real life.

The *Daodejing* is clearly aware of this: "Music and food can attract the attention of passersby, but with the Tao, it often appears to be without any flavor at all. You look for it, but it is so tiny, you cannot see it. You listen carefully, but it is so quiet you cannot hear it. But when using it, it will never be depleted." (Chapter 35)

It becomes obviously apparent, when you talk to people in different industries or when you read management journals and business magazines, that simple and evident principles are ignored far more in real life than you would expect. But it is precisely these simple principles of which we have to continually remind ourselves and make them the guides to our actions. The *Daodejing* says: "My words are very easy to understand and they are very easy to implement. (Nevertheless, it seems that) nobody in the world is really able to understand them and nobody is really able to implement them." (Chapter 70)

Sustainability

Shareholder value and quick profits are often mentioned in one breath. Executives like to please shareholders and boards with immediate returns. Shareholders and boards for their part have a strong interest in hiring and retaining the best teams and reward executives with big bonuses for fast profits. A trend evolved out of this which played a part in the creation of the current crisis, that is, a structural imbalance between short-term and long-term strategies and a twisted approach to shareholder value.

Jack Welch, former CEO of General Electric, is for some the paragon of successful management. Others see him as representing an overly narrow focus on shareholder value. But when asked in an interview with the *Financial Times* in March 2009 about "shareholder value as a strategy", he said that to think of it as a strategy in itself, instead of as the result of successful management, was "the dumbest idea in the world."

Only by matching short-term and long-term profits can you guarantee the health of a company and provide lasting value for all its stakeholders, including the shareholders. It sounds so obvious that I almost feel embarrassed to mention it. But just take a look around you.

In the *Daodejing*, the emphasis is always on adopting a long-term view on agendas and the measures to tackle them. Steps taken with care and consideration have not only immediate effects, but also provide consistency and prosperity for future generations.

The *Daodejing* says: "Something that is established well cannot be uprooted. Something that is firmly embraced cannot be taken away." (Chapter 54)

The *Daodejing* then goes on to explain the relevance of implementation and cultivation of this guideline at every level, from that of the individual, to the family, to the state, to that of the whole world.

Consistency, sustainability and long-term efficiency are at the core of Taoist thought. Make sure that every step is taken with a view to translating theory into real-life practice.

Moderation

The current crisis was not caused by companies. Neither was it triggered by politics. The crisis was caused by people, by their misjudgments and short-sightedness, their conscious decision to depart from the Golden Mean.

It is, of course, impossible to know and anticipate everything. But the real problem is that we are often so intent on attaining something and so convinced we can handle any eventuality, that we knowingly ignore the risks involved for us and everybody around us.

As Warren Buffett said in a talk at the

University of Florida in 1998, avoid business partners or colleagues with high intelligence coupled with a lack of integrity. The *Daodejing's* emphasis on personal development as a major prerequisite for top leaders is not idealistic or unpragmatic. As the financial crisis proves so well, it is very important. Greed and self-conceit can be costly.

At several points in the *Daodejing* you find warnings about knowing when to stop and a call for moderation. "If you know when it is enough, you will not be disgraced." (Chapter 44) "There is no bigger disaster than not knowing when it is enough." (Chapter 46)

Always hitting the right spot

Taoism might not be the first thing coming to mind when your company is heavily affected by a crisis. And a Taoist business orientation is no guarantee for success. But Taoism can provide you with excellent food for thought and strategic advice on whatever task you attempt.

One of the most fundamental Taoist

concepts with a wide range of strategic applications is *wuwei* (non-action). *Wuwei* does not refer to any concrete behavior. It is more like a mathematical variable that constantly has to be filled with life. The same holds true for the Taoist concept of "not holding on to things".

Wuwei refers to always hitting the right spot at the right time. This is of course especially important in terms of avoiding a crisis. But it is equally important in terms of dealing with the consequences when you get hit by one.

It is similar to mountaineering or whitewater kayaking, where you are constantly faced with very demanding situations. Success or failure is not determined only by the level of your skills, but also by how good your instinct and intuition are. You need to be absolutely in touch with yourself. And you have to perfectly blend with your environment. This is what *wuwei* – and Taoism – is all about.

There is a story in the *Zhuangzi* which gives vivid illustration of *wuwei* and at the same time shows what, from a Taoist point of view, is regarded as true mastery of a profession.

Cook Ding was butchering an ox for King Wenhui. The way Ding's hand touched the ox, the way his shoulder leaned against the carcass, the way he placed his foot or used his knee to exert some pressure, and the sounds of the process along with the rhythmic moves of the knife merged into a dance.

King Wenhui was delighted. "Oh, wonderful! How did you achieve such a level of skill?" he asked.

Cook Ding put his knife aside. "What I am fond of," he said, "is the Tao, which is more than just a matter of skill. When I started to butcher oxen, I saw an ox merely as one solid block, but after three years of the work, I no longer saw the ox like that. Today, I approach them with my spirit and do not use my eyes anymore. My senses stop and it is my spirit that begins to move, following the laws of nature. I find the bigger gaps and the larger cavities and simply go along with what I find. I never touch tendons and muscles, let alone the bigger bones.

Good cooks change knives once a year, because

they are cutting, while ordinary cooks change knives each month, because they are chopping. I have been using this knife for nineteen years now. I have butchered thousands of oxen with it, but the blade of my knife looks like it has just come from the grinding stone." (Zhuangzi, chapter 3)

Chapter 8

The Tao and the Global Economic Crisis

Tao Takeaways

- ☯ Be vigilant
- ☯ Build on detail
- ☯ Focus on immediate effects entailing long-term effectiveness
- ☯ Constantly adapt to your environment
- ☯ Take your skills to higher levels

Acknowledgements

If it were not for my publisher and editor Graham Earnshaw, *The Tao of Business* would not have been written. It was he who approached me with the idea of writing this kind of book. He provided me – in a very Taoist way – with many suggestions, always supportive and energizing. For a couple of years, I had tossed around ideas in my head for two books on the *Daodejing*. But the timing and the circumstance were just not right. In this case, it was the perfect match.

I am also very grateful to Hai Benron, General Manager, SEZ China Co. Ltd. and SEZ Asia Pacific, for our conversations and his very helpful suggestions on researching my topics.

Very special thanks go to my wife, Karoline Tschuggnall, PhD, for her patience as well as her support in creating the space I needed for writing. I am also very grateful for our endless discussions on *The Tao of Business* and the suggestions they provided.

I would furthermore like to thank Torsten Weise, Managing Director Weise Verlagsberatung GmbH, Derek Sandhaus, Chief Editor of Earnshaw Books, and Carsten Jäkel, Executive Director W+D Engineering Shanghai, who offered very valuable comments on the manuscript of *The Tao of Business*.

Finally, I would like to personally thank the World Wide Web for providing such a wealth of information. A couple of years back, it would have taken a tremendous amount of time, energy and money to collect the data for this book. And I would probably still be seen roaming libraries doing research for *The Tao of Business*.

Ansgar Gerstner
Shanghai, May, 2009

Selected readings, videos and audio files

Building a Business

Ackermann, Josef. "Der Stellenwert von Corporate Social Responsibility (CSR) in der Deutschen Bank." Speech in Frankfurt a.M., June 10, 2008, www.deutsche-bank. de/presse/de/downloads/CSR_PK_Rede_JA_final_version.pdf.

Bonini, Sheila M. J., Greg Hintz and Lenny T. Mendonca. "Addressing Consumer Concerns about Climate Change." *The McKinsey Quarterly*, March 2008, pp. 0-9.

Bonini, Sheila, Jieh Greeney and Lenny Mendonca. "Assessing the Impact of Societal Issues." A McKinsey Global Survey, *The McKinsey Quarterly*, November 2007, pp. 1-9.

Buffett, Warren. Talk at the University of Florida School of Business, October 15, 1998, www.intelligentinvestorclub. com/seminars/warren-buffett-mba-talk-at-university-of-florida-video.

Burlingham, Bo. *Small Giants: Companies that Choose to Be Great Instead of Big*. London: Penguin Books, 2007.

Corbett, Stephen and others. "Beyond Manufacturing: The Evolution of Lean Production." *The McKinsey Quarterly*, August 2007, pp. 95-105.

"Corporate Social Responsibility: Just Good Business." *The Economist*, January 17, 2008, www.economist.com/special-reports/displaystory.cfm?story_id=10491077.

"Dealing with Dilemmas." *China Economic Review*, June 1, 2002, www.chinaeconomicreview.com/dailybriefing/2002_06_01/Dealing_with_dilemmas.html.

"Does Green Sell in Asia?" A market research report by CatchOn, a Hong Kong based strategic marketing communications consultancy, 2009, pp. 1-27.

Emiliani, M.L. "Cracking the Code of Business." *Management Decision*, 38/2, 2000, pp. 60-79 or for download at www.theclbm.com/papers/ccob.pdf.

"Environmental Protection as a Business Driver." Introduction and links to a 2007 joint study on innovation and the environment by the German Institute for Economic Research, the Fraunhofer Institute for Systems and Innovation Research and Roland Berger Strategy Consultants: www.rolandberger.com/expertise/industries/environmental_technology/2007-06-01-rbsc-pub-Environmental_protection_as_a_business_driver.html.

Flinchbaugh, Jamie. "Connecting Lean and Organizational Learning." Article can be downloaded from the *Lean Learning Center* website: www.leanlearningcenter.com/downloads/Connecting_Lean_and_Organizational_Learning.pdf.

Friedman, Milton. "The Social Responsibility of Business is to Increase its Profits." *The New York Times Magazine*, September 13, 1970.

Gates, Bill. "A New Approach to Capitalism in the 21st Century." World Economic Forum 2008, Davos, Switzerland, January 24, 2008, www.microsoft.com/Presspass/exec/billg/speeches/2008/01-24WEFDavos.mspx.

Glaeser, Edward L. "The Big Three? Try the Small Many."
The New York Times, March 3, 2009, http://economix.
blogs.nytimes.com/2009/03/03/the-big-three-try-the-
small-many/.

Helgesen, Sally. "The Practical Wisdom of Ikujiro Nonaka."
Strategy + Business, issue 53, Winter 2008, www.strat-
egy-business.com/press/article/08407?gko=31376-1876-
27265316.

Hofer, Joachim & Hans Schürmann. "Green-IT: 'Grüne'
Rechner brillieren als Kostenkiller." February 25, 2009,
Handelsblatt, www.handelsblatt.com/technologie/it-inter-
net/gruene-rechner-brillieren-als-kostenkiller;2171447.

Jobs, Steve. "Macworld San Francisco 2007 Keynote Address." www.apple.com/quicktime/qtv/mwsf07/.

Kempkens, Wolfgang. "Wie deutsche Traditionsunterneh-
men die Umwelttechnik entdecken." *Wirtschaftswoche*,
April 15, 2009, http://www.wiwo.de/technik/wie-deut-
sche-traditionsunternehmen-die-umwelttechnik-entdek-
ken-393395/.

Kirdahy, Matthew. "Viva La Workplace Revolution." *Forbes
Magazine*, June 23, 2008, www.forbes.com/2008/06/23/
workplace-rowe-productivity-lead-cx_mk_0623work.html.

Landler, Mark. "Whiff of Reform at Deutsche Bank." *International Herald Tribune*, August 27, 2005, www.iht.com/ar-
ticles/2005/08/26/business/deutsche.php.

Leadbeater, Charles. *The User Innovation Revolution:
How Business Can Unlock the Value of Customers' Ideas.*
NCC – National Consumer Council Publication, Lon-
don, March 2006, http://collections.europarchive.org/

tna/20080804145057/http://www.ncc.org.uk/nccpdf/
poldocs/NCC112ft_innovation_revolution.pdf.

Leadbeater, Charles. "Charles Leadbeater on Innovation."
TED talk, Oxford, England, July 2005, www.ted.com/in-
dex.php/talks/charles_leadbeater_on_innovation.html.

Miller, Matthew. "The World's Richest People: Gates No
Longer World's Richest Man." *Forbes*, March 5, 2008,
www.forbes.com/2008/03/05/buffett-worlds-richest-
cx_mm_0229buffetrichest.html.

Nocera, Joe. "It's not the Bonus Money. It's the Principle."
The New York Times, January 31, 2009, www.nytimes.
com/2009/01/31/business/31nocera.html.

Oberhäuser, Notker. "Lernen von den Hidden Champions."
Handelsblatt, November 2, 2006, www.handelsblatt.com/
unternehmen/mittelstand_aktuell/lernen-von-den-hid-
den-champions;1158790.

"One-on-one with Warren Buffett." Nightly Business Report,
extended interview. *PBS*, January 22, 2009, www.pbs.org/
nbr/site/research/learnmore/090122_buffett/.

Price, Colin. "Business and the Art of Transformation." *The
McKinsey Quarterly*, August 2006, pp. 4-5

"Remarks of Bill Gates – Harvard Commencement." *The
Harvard University Gazette Online*, June 7, 2007, www.news.
harvard.edu/gazette/2007/06.14/99-gates.html.

"Rethinking the Social Responsibility of Business." A Reason
debate featuring Milton Friedman, John Mackey, and
T.J. Rodgers, October 2005, www.reason.com/news/
show/32239.html

Rose, Charlie. "An Hour with Warren Buffett, Bill Gates & Melinda Gates." June 26, 2006, www.charlierose.com/view/interview/345.

Stiglitz, Joseph. Speech at the Financial Services Committee Hearing on Financial Regulation, United States House of Representatives. October 21, 2008, www.house.gov/apps/list/hearing/financialsvcs_dem/hr102108.shtml.

Taleb, Nassim. *The Black Swan: The Impack of the Highly Improbable.* London: Penguin Books, 2007.

Willershausen, Florian. "Grüne Energie treibt die Wirtschaft an." *karriere.de*, July 7, 2007, www.karriere.de/beruf/gruene-energie-treibt-die-wirtschaft-an-6465/.

Womack, Jim. "The Power of Purpose, Process, and People." A LEI (Lean Enterprise Institute) webinar originally presented May 1, 2008, www.lean.org/Events/WebinarHome.cfm.

"'You've Got to Find What You Love', Jobs says." *Stanford Report*, June 14, 2005, http://news-service.stanford.edu/news/2005/june15/jobs-061505.html.

Competing in the Marketplace

"As Layoffs Spread, Innovative Alternatives May Soften the Blow." *Knowledge@Wharton*, November 26, 2008, http://knowledge.wharton.upenn.edu/article.cfm?articleid=2106.

"Avon's Andrea Jung: 'You Will Stand on Our Shoulders'." *Knowledge@Wharton*, January 14, 2005, http://knowledge.wharton.upenn.edu/article.cfm?articleid=1095&specialid=26.

Ayers, Andrea J. "Executives Have No Idea What Customers Want." *Forbes*, March 10, 2009, www.forbes.com/2009/03/10/consumers-executives-disconnect-leadership-managing-convergys.html?partner=alerts.

"Bill Gates and Steve Jobs." An Interview by Kara Swisher and Walt Mossberg at *All Things Digital*, *The Wall Street Journal* Executive Conference, May 30, 2007, http://d5.allthingsd.com/20070530/d5-gates-jobs-interview/.

Bonini, Sheila M.J., Kerrin McKillop and Lenny T. Mendonca. "The Trust Gap between Consumers and Corporations." *The McKinsey Quarterly*, May 2007, pp. 7-10.

Bonini, Sheila M.J., Kerrin McKillop and Lenny T. Mendonca. "What Consumers Expect from Companies." *The McKinsey Quarterly*, May 2007, pp. 11-17.

Brooker, Katrina. "It Took A Lady To Save Avon." *Fortune*, October 15, 2001, http://money.cnn.com/magazines/fortune/fortune_archive/2001/10/15/311507/index.htm.

Carroué, Laurent. "US Car Industry Runs out of Gas." *Le Monde Diplomatique*, English on-line edition, March 2009.

"Chasing the Rabbit." Steven J. Spear interviewed by Mark Graban. *LeanBlog* Podcast number 58, January 18, 2009, www.leanblog.org/2009/01/leanblog-podcast-58-steven-j-spear.html.

Cho, Fujio. "Re-inventing Toyota." Transcript of presentation at "Management Briefing Seminars 2004", conference organized by CAR (Center for Automotive Research) in Traverse City, MI, August 4, 2004, www.cargroup.org/mbs2004/documents/ChoTraversespeech-handout.pdf.

Corkindale, Gill. "How to Manage Conflict." Harvard Business Radio, IdeaCast Episode 71, November 29, 2007, www.hbsp.harvard.edu/b01/en/misc/ideacast/archives_hbrideacast_pg5.jhtml.

Day, Peter. "The Car Industry." *BBC Radio 4*, June 28, 2007, www.bbc.co.uk/radio4/news/inbusiness/inbusiness_20070628.shtml.

Deutsch, Claudia H. "A Woman to Be Chief at PepsiCo." *The New York Times*, August 15, 2006, www.nytimes.com/2006/08/15/business/15pepsi.html?ex=1313294400&en=49781154fbb92198&ei=5088&partner=rssnyt&emc=rss.

Emiliani, M.L. "Origins of Lean Management in America: The Role of Connecticut Businesses." *Journal of Management History*, Vol. 12, No. 2, 2006, pp. 167-184 or for download at www.lean.org/Community/Registered/ArticleDocuments/lean%20in%20conn.pdf.

"The Enterprise of the Future." The IBM Global CEO Study 2008. Can be obtained via www-935.ibm.com/services/us/gbs/bus/html/ceostudy2008.html.

"Executive Feature: Fujio Cho." Video on *CNBC*, April 7, 2008, www.cnbc.com/id/15840232?video=704901901.

Fisher, Anne B. "Book & Business; Stuck in Reverse." Review of Maryann Keller's *Rude Awakening: The Rise, Fall, and Struggle for Recovery of General Motors. The New York Times*, October 29, 1989, http://query.nytimes.com/gst/fullpage.html?res=950DEEDA113FF93AA15753C1A96F948260.

"Flexibility: The Answer to Burnout." *BusinessWeek*, Septem-

ber 20, 1999, www.businessweek.com/archives/1999/
b3647148.arc.htm.

Frankel, Barbara. "Pepsico's Indra Nooyi 'I Am a Walking
Example of Diversity'." *DiversityInc*, May 2008, pp. 38-45.

"Genuine, not Just Generous." In the *IBM Global CEO Study
2009*. Somers, NY: IBM Global Business Services, pp. 59-69.

"Glass Ceiling? Part I, II, III." Interview with Andrea Jung
by Stephen Adler. *BusinessWeek*, January 16, 2007, http://
feedroom.businessweek.com/?fr_story=9c7f520596c9b69d
0955f1792f9e0d1841bcde53&rf=sitemap.

"GM's Commitment to the American People." Full-page
open letter in *Automotive News*, December 8, 2008,
available also at www.autonews.com/assets/PDF/
CA59166128.PDF.

Green, Gavin. "Interview Rick Wagoner: No More Mr. Nice
Guy." *Motor Trend*, June 2006, pp. 90-92, 94 or www.
motortrend.com/features/112_0606_rick_wagoner_gen-
eral_motors/index.html.

Hamel, Gary and Liisa Välikangas. "The Quest for Resil-
ience." *Harvard Business Review OnPoint Article*, September
1, 2003, pp. 0 14.

"How China's Companies Can Manage the Pain of Layoffs."
Knowledge@Wharton, March 4, 2009, www.knowledgeat-
wharton.com.cn/index.cfm?fa=viewfeature&articleid=199
9&languageid=1.

"Indra Nooyi Discusses Diversity, Inclusion and Mentoring
at PepsiCo." Indra Nooyi on "Women in Business" at the
2008 Catalyst Awards Conference, New York City. Cornell

University, Department of Applied Economics and Management. *Eclip* at http://eclips.cornell.edu/interviewLecture.do?id=576&clipID=12288&tab=TabClipPage.

"Jim Collins: How Great Companies Turn Crisis into Opportunity." Interview by Jennifer Reingold. *Fortune Magazine*, January 22, 2009, http://money.cnn.com/2009/01/15/news/companies/Jim_Collins_Crisis.fortune/index.htm.

"Job Survival Advice: Don't Fear the Whitewater." *Knowledge@Wharton*, November 12, 2008, http://knowledge.wharton.upenn.edu/article.cfm?articleid=2085.

Keller, Maryann N. "Dull at Any Speed: GM Never Learned to Shift Gears." *The Washington Post*, June 12, 2005, p. B01 or www.washingtonpost.com/wp-dyn/content/article/2005/06/11/AR2005061100180.html.

Langfitt, Frank. "GM Makes Case for Bailout with Ad." Podcast on NPR website, www.npr.org/templates/story/story.php?storyId=97973461.

"Lessons in Business Agility." A podversation with Michael Hugos. IBM Cognos Software podcast, episode no 2, no date given. Downloaded from www.cognos.com.

"李嘉诚讲述: 50年经营哲学." 《首席执行官》, December 12, 2008, http://ceo.icxo.com/html-news/2008/12/24/1345661.htm.

"聆听大师的声音－李嘉诚为长江师生传授"管理艺术"全景实录." Transcript of Li Ka-shing lecture on the art of management plus questions and answers session at Shantou University (汕头大学), June 28, 2005. 《长江－*Cheung Kong*》 magazine, August 20, 2005, pp. 12-17. The magazine can be downloaded from the Cheung Kong Graduate School of

Business website: www.ckgsb.com/download/index.aspx.

Matthews, Carole. "The Real Cost of Layoffs." *Inc.*, July 2002, www.inc.com/articles/2002/07/24434.html.

Maynard, Micheline. "G.M.'s Latest Great Green Hope Is a Tall Order." *The New York Times*, November 22, 2008, www.nytimes.com/2008/11/22/business/22volt. html?pagewanted=1&_r=2&sq=chevrolet%20volt&st=cse &scp=1.

Morss, Ruth. "Creative Approaches to Layoffs." *Salary.com*, www.salary.com/careers/layouthtmls/crel_display_no-cat_Ser17_Par49.html.

Nihara, Hiroaki. "The Skills of the Best Managers at Superior Companies." English translation of Japanese original, reprinted from *Bungei Syunjyu*. *RIETI – Research Institute of Economy, Trade & Industry*, September 2002, www.rieti. go.jp/en/papers/contribution/niihara/01.html.

Nohria, Nitin & Bridget Gurtler. "Li Ka-shing." Case study, *Harvard Business School*, rev. December 19, 2005, pp. 1-12.

"PepsiCo President Charts Path to Diversity and Success." Article on Indra Nooyi's speech at MIT Sloan School of Management, February 28, 2006, http://mitsloan.mit. edu/newsroom/2006-nooyi.php.

Reynolds, Alan. "The Truth about those Bonus Billions." *Forbes*, February 10, 2009, www.forbes.com/2009/02/10/ billion-dollar-bonuses-opinions-contributors_0210_alan_ reynolds.html.

Rigby, Darrell. "Look Before You Lay Off: Downsizing in a Downturn Can Do More Harm than Good." *Harvard*

Business Review, April 1, 2002, pp. 1-3.

Rubin, Harriet. "Sexism." *Condé Nast Portfolio*, April 2008, www.portfolio.com/executives/features/2008/03/17/ Sexism-in-the-Workplace.

Sackmann, Sonja A. "Toyota Motor Corporation: Eine Fallstudie aus unternehmenskultureller Perspektive." Bertelsmann-Stiftung, 2007, pp. 1-43, www.bertelsmann-stiftung. de/cps/rde/xbcr/bst/xcms_bst_dms_13047_13048_2.pdf.

Sheahan, Peter. "Companies Can Benefit from Employees Sharing Positive Experiences." *China Economic Review*, September 2008, www.chinaeconomicreview.com/ cer/2008_09/Companies_can_benefit_from_employees_ sharing_positive_experiences.html.

Surowiecki, James. "It's the Workforce, Stupid!" *The New Yorker*, April 30, 2007, www.newyorker.com/talk/ financial/2007/04/30/070430ta_talk_surowiecki.

Taylor III, Alex. "Rick Wagoner Tries to Catch a Falling Knife – and Fails." *Fortune Magazine*, July 15, 2008, http:// money.cnn.com/2008/07/15/news/companies/taylor_ gm.fortune/index.htm?source=yahoo_quote.

Taylor, Alex III. "Toyota: The Birth of the Prius." *Fortune*, February 21, 2006, http://money.cnn.com/2006/02/17/ news/companies/mostadmired_fortune_toyota/index. htm.

Thompson, Arthur A. and John E. Gamble. Case 35, "Southwest Airlines: Culture, Values, and Operating Practices." In Arthur A. Thompson, Alonzo J.

Strickland and John E. Gamble. *Crafting and Executing*

Strategy: The Quest for Competitive Advantage – Concepts and Cases. New York: McGraw-Hill, 2004, pp. C-636 – C-664, or www.suu.edu/faculty/johnsonr/4950/05_Southwest. pdf.

"Thoughts of Li Ka-shing." Interview with Li Ka-shing by Tim W. Ferguson and Vivian Wai-Yin Kwok. *Forbes*, December 29, 2006, www.forbes.com/2006/12/29/li-ka-shing-biz-cx_tf_vk_1229qanda.html.

"Toyota's Endeavors for Sustainable Mobility." Presentation by Fujio Cho at the 37th St. Gallen Symposium, June 2, 2007, http://streamstudio.world-television.com/ CCUIv3/frameset.aspx?ticket=31-44-5247&browser=ns-1-10-0-10-0&target=en-default-&status=ondemand&stream =rm-video-100.

Vogel, David. "CSR Doesn't Pay." *Forbes*, October 16, 2008, www.forbes.com/2008/10/16/csr-doesnt-pay-lead-cor-prespons08-cx_dv_1016vogel.html.

Wheary, Jennifer. "U.S. is Losing Education Race with China." *Newsday*, September 1, 2008, www.newsday.com/ news/opinion/ny-opwhe055789535aug05,0,5415291.story.

Winston, Andrew. "Greener B-Schools, Greener Employ-ees." Harvard Business Online's Leading Green, May 30, 2008, http://blogs.harvardbusiness.org/leading-green/2008/05/greener-bschools-greener-emplo-1.html.

Being the Boss

"About Virgin." Company information from the Virgin Group website: www.virgin.com/AboutVirgin/ WhatWeAreAbout/WhatWeAreAbout.aspx?L3_

GenericContent_NavigateToPage=1.

"American Recovery and Reinvestment." Remarks of
President-Elect Barack Obama as prepared for deliv-
ery, January 8, 2009, www.whitehouse.gov/agenda/
economy/. His speech at George Mason University
can be watched at www.cbsnews.com/video/watch/
?id=4707795n%3fsource=search_video.

"Anne Mulcahy on Women in Business." Interview by
Chrystia Freeland. *Financial Times*, May 9, 2007, www.
ft.com/cms/8a38c684-2a26-11dc-9208-000b5df10621.
html?_i_referralObject=431474578&_i_referrer=rss.

Bielak, Debby, Sheila M.J. Bonini and Jeremy M. Oppenheim.
"CEOs on Strategy and Social Issues." *The McKinsey Quarterly*, October 2007, pp. 0-8.

Brady, Diane. "Indra Nooyi: Keeping Cool in Hot Water."
BusinessWeek, June 11, 2007, www.businessweek.com/
magazine/content/07_24/b4038067.htm.

Bruch, Heike and Sumantra Ghoshal. "Beware the Busy
Manager." *Harvard Business Review OnPoint Article*, pp.
0-10.

Chandler, Clay. "Full Speed Ahead: Toyota CEO Fujio Cho
Is Driving the Japanese Automaker to New Heights — and
Straight Past the Competition." *Fortune*, February 7, 2005,
http://money.cnn.com/magazines/fortune/fortune_ar-
chive/2005/02/07/8250430/index.htm.

"A Conversation with former CEO of GE Jack Welch," part 1
and 2, October 23 and 24, 2001. A Charlie Rose interview,
www.charlierose.com.

Collins, Jim. "Dialogue and Debate, Not Consensus." Audio accessible at www.jimcollins.com/hall/index.html.

Collins, Jim. "The 10 Greatest CEOs of All Time." *Fortune*, July 21, 2003, http://money.cnn.com/magazines/fortune/fortune_archive/2003/07/21/346095/index.htm.

Daft, Richard L. *Management*. Beijing: Harcourt Brace & Company Asia PTE, 2000 (5th edition).

Day, Peter. "'Mr Toyota' Is Shy About Being No 1." *BBC Radio 4* and *BBC World Service*, June 25, 2007, http://news.bbc.co.uk/1/hi/business/6237110.stm.

Dorgan, Stephen J. and John Dowdy. "How Good Management Raises Productivity." *The McKinsey Quarterly*, November 2002, No 4, pp. 14-17.

"Exploring Business's Social Contract: An Interview with Daniel Yankelovich." *The McKinsey Quarterly*, May 2007, pp. 65-73.

"Global Survey of Business Executives." *The McKinsey Quarterly*, January 2006, pp. 1-10.

Greenberg, Margaret. "An Interview with Toyota University's Mike Morrison." November 14, 2007, http://pospsych.com/news/margaret-greenberg/20071114480.

Jungclausen, John F. "Momente der Entscheidung: Der Mann als Marke." *Die Zeit*, September 25, 2003, www.zeit.de/2003/40/Branson_2fVirgin.

Kelleher, Herb. "A Culture of Commitment." *Leader to Leader*, 1997, pp. 20-24 or www.leadertoleader.org/knowledgecenter/journal.aspx?ArticleID=143.

Levine, Greg. "Cho: Despite Success, Toyota Sees 'Crisis' and 'Fear'." *Forbes*, August 5, 2004, www.forbes.com/ 2004/08/05/0805autofacescan02.html.

"Life at 30,000 Feet." Interview with Richard Branson by Chris Anderson. *TED*, March 2007, www.ted.com/index. php/talks/richard_branson_s_life_at_30_000_feet.html.

"Richard Branson, Founder, Virgin." Richard Branson interviewed by Todd Benjamin. *CNN International*, September 10, 2007, http://edition.cnn.com/2007/BUSI-NESS/09/06/boardroom.branson/index.html.

Rifkin, Glenn. "How Richard Branson Works Magic." *Strategy + Business*, Fourth Quarter 1998, www.strategy-business.com/press/16635507/13416.

Schwartz, Jonathan."Transparenz: Wer bloggt, der führt." *Harvard Business Manager*, February 12, 2009, www.harvardbusinessmanager.de/heft/artikel/a-605410.html.

"View from the Top: Anne Mulcahy, Chairman and CEO, Xerox." Speech at Stanford Graduate School of Business, December 1, 2004, www.gsb.stanford.edu/news/headlines/vftt_mulcahy.shtml.

Wihofszki, Oliver. "Fujio Cho: Mächtiger Gesprächspartner." *Financial Times Deutschland*, December 28, 2006, www. ftd.de/koepfe/:Kopf-des-Tages-Fujio-Cho-M%E4chtiger-Gespr%E4chspartner/145228.html.

Managing a Team

Buckingham, Edward. "When Firms Sponsor Their Star Employees' EMBA Educations, Both Sides Stand to Gain." *China Economic Review*, July 2008, www.chinaeconomicreview.com/cer/2008_07/When_firms_sponsor_their_star_employees%E2%80%99_EMBA_educations_both_sides_stand_to_gain.html.

Catmull, Ed. "Teamwork: Kollektive Kreativität bei Pixar." *Harvard Business Manager*, February 24, 2009, www.harvardbusinessmanager.de/heft/artikel/a-607820.html.

Collins, Jim. "Trying to Motivate People Is a Waste of Time." Audio accessible at www.jimcollins.com/hall/index.html.

Culbert, Samuel A. "Get Rid of the Performance Review!" *The Wall Street Journal*, October 20, 2008, http://online.wsj.com/article/SB122426318874844933.html.

Donlon, J.P. Interview with Herb Kelleher, July 1, 1999, www.chiefexecutive.net/ME2/Audiences/dirmod.asp?sid=&nm=&type=Publishing&mod=Publications::Article&mid=8F3A7027421841978F18BE895F87F791&AudID=257093CD337F495B86A6A07046702F8C&tier=4&id=1EA0DEE20524400E83E7FFFA89A7D0EB.

Fernandez, Juan Antonio & Laurie Underwood. *China CEO: Voices of Experience from 20 International Business Leaders.* Singapore: John Wiley & Sons, 2006.

Field, Anne. "Moving from 'Me' to 'We'." *Harvard Management Update*, January 16, 2009, http://blogs.harvardbusiness.org/hmu/2009/01/moving-from-me-to-we.php?cm_mmc=npv-_-MGMT_TIP-_-JAN_2009-_-MTOD0116.

"Finders Keepers: Finding Employees Is Only Half the Battle; Retaining Them Can Be a Much Bigger Challenge." *China Economic Review*, January 2008, www.chinaeconomicreview.com/cer/2008_01/Finders_keepers.html.

Goleman, Daniel, Richard Boyatzis and Annie McKee. "Best of HBR on Emotionally Intelligent Leadership, 2nd Edition." *Harvard Business Review*, September 1, 2008, pp. 0-50.

Gosset, Steve. "Sometimes You Do Have to Fire People." *Harvard Business Review*, October 1, 1999, pp. 1-5.

"Herb Kelleher on Leadership." Interview with Herb Kelleher by Brian McCormick for *LeaderNetwork*, September 1, 2007. Audio file can be downloaded from www.leadernetwork.org/leadership_podcast.rss.

"How to Inspire Workers in Tough Times." *BusinessWeek*, January 23, 2009, www.businessweek.com/managing/content/jan2009/ca20090123_155726.htm.

Jones, Dell. "Let People Know where They Stand, Welch Says: Ranking Workers Pays, Former GE Chief Says." *USA Today*, April 18, 2005, www.usatoday.com/educate/college/careers/Advice/advice4-18-05.htm.

"Kelleher: Agent of Airline Change," May 13, 2008. A Smithsonian video, www.nasm.si.edu/events/lectures/webcast/archive.cfm.

Livingston, Sterling J. "Pygmalion in Management." *Harvard Business Review* OnPoint, September 1, 2002, pp. 1-11.

"Maritz Poll: Will Poor Managers Harm Companies by Fostering Bad Customer Experience?" www.maritz.com/Maritz-Poll/2007/Maritz-Poll-Will-Poor-Managers-Harm-

Companies-by-Fostering-Bad-Customer-Experiences.aspx

Spear, Steven J. "Learning to Lead at Toyota." *Harvard Business Review*, *OnPoint* article, May 2004, pp. 0-10.

Sutton, Robert. "Building the Civilized Workplace." *The McKinsey Quarterly*, May 2007, No 2, pp. 47-55.

"Unlocking the DNA of the Adaptable Workforce." The IBM Global Human Capital Study 2008. Somers, NY: IBM Global Services, 2008.

Welch, Jack. His official website on "differentiation": www.welchway.com/Principles/Differentiation.aspx.

Creating Workplaces

"Dilbert Is Right, Says Gallup Study: A national employee survey confirms that uncomfortable work environments do make for disgruntled employees." *Gallup Management Journal*, April 13, 2006, http://gmj.gallup.com/content/22381/Dilbert-Right-Says-Gallup-Study.aspx.

"A Dream Workplace." Video on DreamWorks Animation, *Fortune*, January 21, 2009, http://money.cnn.com/video/ft/A.

Haslam, Alex and Craig Knight. "Your Space or Mine." FX Magazine, September 2006, p. 57.

"The Impact of Office Design on Business Performance." Published by the Commission for Architecture & the Built Environment and the British Council for Offices, May 2005. The full report can be downloaded from www.cabe.org.uk/publications/the-impact-of-office-design-on-business-performance.

"Productivity and Office Design: Beyond Feng Shui." American Management Association, e-Newsletter, September
2006, www.amanet.org/performance-profits/editorial.
cfm?Ed=340.

"The U.S. Workplace Survey". The Gensler Design + Performance Index, July 2008, www.gensler.com/#viewpoint/
publications.

WBDG Productive Committee. "Productive." Whole Building Design Guide (WBDG), April 30, 2008, www.wbdg.
org/design/productive.php.

Dealing with Stress

Cryer, Bruce, Rollin McCraty and Doc Childre. "Pull the
Plug on Stress." *Harvard Business Review*, July 1, 2003, pp.
0-7.

Debaise, Colleen. "Work & Life: Avoiding Stress Eating."
The Wall Street Journal, July 10, 2008, http://online.wsj.
com/article/SB121563563957540335.html.

"Doping im Büro: Manager auf Speed." *Manager-Magazin*,
February 12, 2009, www.manager-magazin.de/koepfe/ar-
tikel/0,2828,607267,00.html.

Dusen, Allison Van. "Best Workplace Stress Relievers."
Forbes.com, May 2, 2007, www.forbes.com/2007/05/01/
stress-health-office-forbeslife-cx_avd_0502stress.html.

Kleinschmidt, Carola. "Stress im Job: Angestellte arbeiten
sich krank." *Spiegel Online*, January 3, 2007, www.spiegel.
de/wissenschaft/mensch/0,1518,455382,00.html.

McFarland, Jennifer. "High-Performance Prison." *Harvard*

Management Update, June 1, 2001, pp. 1-3.

"A Positive Approach to Workplace Stress." Interview with Shelley E. Taylor by Jennifer Robinson for the *Gallup Management Journal*. August 16, 2007, www.greatmanagement. org/articles/292/1/A-Positive-Approach-to-Workplace-Stress/Page1.html.

Ruiz, Rebecca. "Stress-Relieving Workouts." *Forbes.com*, October 31, 2007, www.forbes.com/health/2007/10/30/stress-exercise-workout-forbeslife-cx_rr_1031health.html.

Storch, Maja. "Coaching: Wie Manager entspannen lernen." *Manager-Magazin*, February 18, 2009, www.manager-magazin.de/harvard/0,2828,608243,00.html.

"Stress ... at Work." DHHS (NIOSH – National Institute for Occupational Safety and Health of the U.S. Department of Health and Human Services) publication No. 99-101, 1999, www.cdc.gov/niosh/atwork.html.

The Tao and the Global Economic Crisis

Aldrick, Philip. "UBS Launches Radical Overhaul of Bonus System." *Telegraph.co.uk*, November 17, 2008, www.telegraph.co.uk/finance/newsbysector/banksandfinance/3473277/UBS-launches-radical-overhaul-of-bonus-system.html.

Barton, Dominic, Yi Wang and Mei Ye. "A Chinese View on Governance and the Financial Crisis: An Interview with ICBC's Chairman." *McKinsey Quarterly*, March 2009, www.mckinseyquarterly.com/Governance/Leadership/A_Chinese_view_of_governance_and_the_financial_crisis__An_ interview_with_ICBCs_chairman_2315?gp=1.

Cohan, William D. "The Wall Street Bonus in Re-
    treat." *Fortune*, March 16, 2009, http://money.cnn.
    com/2009/03/16/news/companies/bonus_retreat.for-
    tune/index.htm.

Collingwood, Harris. "The Earnings Game: Everyone Plays,
    Nobody Wins." *Harvard Business Review* OnPoint Article,
    March 1, 2002, pp. 5-12.

Cossin, Didier. "Superstar Bank Leaders Pull up Lame."
    Forbes, May 8, 2009, www.forbes.com/2009/05/08/bank-
    ing-ubs-management-personal-finance-guru-insight-secu-
    ritization-cmbs.html?partner=alerts.

Geoghegan, Thomas. "Infinite Debt: How Unlimited Inter-
    est Rates Destroyed the Economy." *Harper's Magazine*,
    April 2009, pp. 32-39.

Guerrera, Francesco. "A Need to Reconnect." *FT.com*, March
    12, 2009, www.ft.com/cms/s/0/822ed110-0f3d-11de-ba10-
    0000779fd2ac.html.

"Half-a-Million Job Cuts: Is There a Strategy Behind
    the Layoffs?" *Knowledge@Wharton*, February 4, 2009,
    http://knowledge.wharton.upenn.edu/article.
    cfm?articleid=2154.

"Jack Welch Elaborates: Shareholder Value." *Business-
    Week*, March 16, 2009, www.businessweek.com/bw-
    daily/dnflash/content/mar2009/db20090316_630496.
    htm?campaign_id=rss_daily.

Kovacevich, Richard. Speech about the causes of the finan-
    cial crisis at SIEPR (Stanford Institute for Economic Policy

Research) Economic Summit 2009, March 13, 2009, http://siepr.stanford.edu/.

Leadbeater, Charles, James Meadway et al. *Attacking the Recession: How Innovation Can Fight the Downturn*. NESTA (The National Endowment for Science, Technology and the Arts) discussion paper, London, December 2008, www.nesta.org.uk/assets/Uploads/pdf/Interim-report/attacking_the_recession_discussion_paper_NESTA.pdf.

Nocera, Joe. "Risk Mismanagement." *The New York Times*, January 2, 2009, www.nytimes.com/2009/01/04/magazine/04risk-t.html?_r=1.

The Progressive Magazine interview with Dean Baker by Matthew Rothschild on Baker's book, *Plunder and Blunder: The Rise and Fall of the Bubble Economy*. March 9, 2009, www.learnoutloud.com/Podcast-Directory/Politics/Liberal-Politics/The-Progressive-Radio-Show-Podcast/7333#3.

"Reporting on Risk: A Q&A with the World's First Chief Risk Officer." IBM Performance Perspectives, Information Technology, March 30, 2009, www.cognos.com/newsletter/finance/st_090330_02.html.

"Taleb on the Financial Crisis." Russ Roberts interviews Nassim Taleb. *EconTalk*, March 15, 2009, www.econtalk.org/archives/2009/03/taleb_on_the_fi.html.

Thompson, Christopher and Steve Culp. "After G-20, Emerging-Market Banks May Inherit the Earth." *Forbes*, April 1, 2009, www.forbes.com/2009/04/01/banks-emerging-markets-leadership-governance-g20.html?partner=alerts.

Wieser, Christina & Markus Oberrauter.

"Vorstandsvergütung und Ausschüttungspolitik der ATX Unternehmen 2008." A survey published by the Austrian Chamber of Labor in April 2009. It can be downloaded from their website: http://www.arbeiterkammer.at/online/managergagen-steigen-weiter-47848.html.

General

Gerstner, Ansgar. "Das Buch *Laozi*: Übersetzungen mehrerer chinesischer Ausgaben mit Kommentaren." Saarbrücken: VDM Verlag Dr. Müller, 2008.

《庄子今注今译》，上下册。陈鼓应注释。1975年初版。台北：台湾商务印书馆，1994年。

Last access to given internet resources May 12, 2009.

Index

More Earnshaw Books for your China reading pleasure.
For details, see

www.earnshawbooks.com

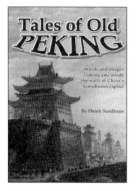

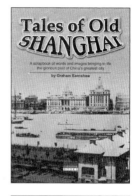

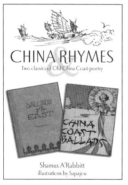

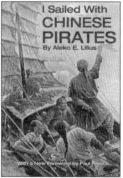

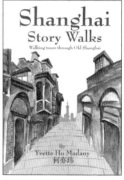

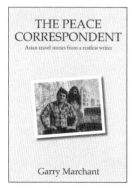

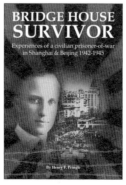